T H E
ATLAS *of*
Endangered
RESOURCES

Steve Pollock

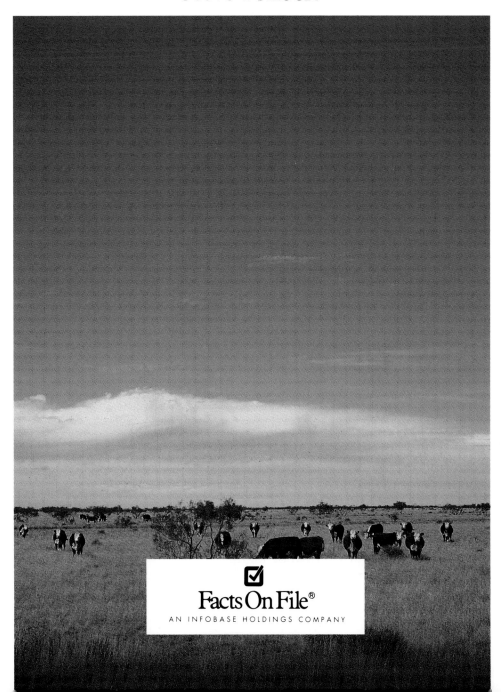

Facts On File®
AN INFOBASE HOLDINGS COMPANY

The Atlas of Endangered Resources

Facts On File, Inc.
460 Park Avenue South
New York NY 10016
USA

Library of Congress Cataloging-in-Publication Data
Pollock, Steve (Stephen Thomas)
    The atlas of endangered resources / Steve Pollock.
       p.   cm.
    Includes bibliographical references and index.
    ISBN 0-8160-3284-X
    1. Natural resources—Maps for children.   2. Man—Influence on
nature—Maps for children.   [1. Natural resources—Maps.
2. Man—influence on nature—Maps.   3. Atlases.]   I. Title.
G1046.G3P65 1995   <G&M>
333.7' .022'3—dc20   94-32549
                                                    CIP
                                                  MAP AC

Facts On File books are available at special discounts when purchased in
bulk quantities for businesses, associations, institutions or sales promotions.
Please call our Special Sales Department in New York at 212/683-2244
or 800/322-8755.

10 9 8 7 6 5 4 3 2 1

First published in the United States by Facts On File in 1995.
First published in the UK in 1995 by Belitha Press Limited.
Copyright in this format © Belitha Press 1995
Text copyright © Steve Pollock 1995
Illustrations copyright © Belitha Press 1995
Cartography copyright © Creative Cartography 1989
Black and white illustrations by Cat & Mouse Design Consultants, London
Miniature maps by Eugene Fleury
Editor: Claire Edwards
Designed by Cat & Mouse Design Consultants, London
Consultant: Steve Watts
Printed in Singapore for Imago

Picture acknowledgments: Ancient Art and Architecture Collection: 40 top;
Camera Press: 20 top and 26 top; Bruce Coleman Ltd: 14 bottom Gunter
Ziesler, 21 top Wayne Lankinen, 22 bottom Steven C Kaufman, 38 top John
Fennell, 39 bottom Gerald Cubitt, 52 top CB and DW Frith, 56 bottom Janos
Jurka, 58 top Ken Balcomb; FLPA: 44 top Chris Mattison, 46 bottom
L Vigliotti/Panda; Greenpeace Communications: 33 bottom NMFS; Robert
Harding Picture Library: 21 center; The Hutchison Library: 14 top right,
16 top, 18 bottom, 50 bottom; Magnum Photos: cover and 48 top Donald
McCullin, 30 bottom Leonard Freed, 40 bottom Steve McCurry, 46 top Hiroji
Kubota, 48 bottom Paul Fusco; NASA: 4; Novosti: 42 bottom; Oxford Scientific
Films: 54 top Daniel J Fox; Planet Earth Pictures: 58 bottom K A Puttock;
Science Photo Library: 28 bottom Martin Bond; Frank Spooner Pictures:
7 top Chip Hires/Gamma, 29 center Christophe Chermette/Gamma, 30 top
Alexis Duclos/Gamma, 32 bottom Eddy, 34 bottom Micozzi, 42 top Gilles
Saussier, 49 Kaku Kurita/Gamma, 54 bottom Brecelj-Hodalic/Gamma; Still
Pictures: cover and 20 bottom David Hoffman, cover, 8, 10 bottom,
14 top left, 28 top, 29 bottom, 34 top, 36 top, 39 top, 50 top and 52 bottom
Mark Edwards, cover and 56 top Al Grillo, 5 top WWF/Mauri Rautkari, 5 bottom
John Maier, 6 David Drain, 9 Heldur Netocny, 10 top Carsten Rahbek, 22 top
and 26 bottom B & C Alexander, 24 top and 33 top Andre Maslennikov,
24 bottom Argus, 36 bottom Renson Genevieve/BIOS, 38 bottom Chris
Caldicott, 44 bottom Jorgen Schytte; Topham Picture Point: title page and
20 center, 16 bottom; TRIP: 32 top V Sidoropolev.

CONTENTS

INTRODUCTION

Resources refers to everything in the natural environment around us that we are able to use in some way. The food we eat is a resource. It gives our bodies the energy to live. The land we grow the food on is also a resource. We use resources such as iron and rubber to build a car, and we use mineral resources to provide the energy to drive it. Energy and resources are both essential to us and have a very special relationship. Energy exists in many of the resources we use, and we have **exploited** the Earth's resources by using this energy.

ENERGY AND RESOURCES

There is one important difference between energy and resources. Most energy ultimately comes from the sun and is eventually transferred into space. Although it can never be lost, it can also never be reused. Resources such as water, soil and the air we breathe can all be recycled and become part of something else. The carbon atoms that are part of someone today may have been part of the body of a dinosaur living millions of years ago. But the energy from the sun, which helped grow the plants the dinosaur ate, has long since disappeared into space.

▲ *We must learn to use the Earth's resources in a sustainable way if we do not wish to harm our planet.*

FOOD AND HEAT

Energy is available to humans in several forms. For example, it comes from the food we eat. The science of growing food is called agriculture. Agriculture has freed many people from simply surviving and allowed them to develop complex civilizations.

When early humans discovered fire, they also found a way of releasing heat energy. They did this by burning wood – and the forests and woodlands of the world have been cut down ever since to provide fuel.

FROM WOOD TO COAL

In the 1700s people in some countries started to burn coal instead of wood. In developed countries this happened because of a shortage of wood. In Great Britain it became increasingly cheaper for people to find ways to dig out coal from the ground and use this as a fuel. They used it not only for heating, but also for industry. For the same reason, people began to build using steel made from iron ore, a natural resource dug from the ground,

▲ *Barley is a source of food energy.*

instead of using wood. The first **technological revolution** was beginning, and newly **industrialized** countries began to emerge.

In the United States coal mining began much later because there was plenty of wood available in the North American forests.

▲ *Wood is still an important resource for building and papermaking.*

5

COST VS. ENVIRONMENT

As more and more countries in Europe became industrialized, their economies relied less on agriculture and more on manufacturing. They turned their resources into products, which they sold to one another to earn money. Today money has become a resource in its own right, but it is important to remember that money and wealth depend on the availability and exploitation of natural resources.

The way we use resources is affected by how much they cost. For example, oil is cheaper to exploit than some alternative energy resources. But exploiting oil sources can damage the environment, and there is a cost in repairing that damage. So people should take into account not just the cost of the resource, but also the cost of repairing environmental damage that results from its use.

RESOURCE MANAGEMENT

Wherever people are they have to use resources, and they continue to do so even though their use sometimes damages the environment. But if people plan and manage resources carefully, they can use them effectively and efficiently in what is called a sustainable way. This means that people take what they need for the present and plan ahead for the

RENEWABLE AND NON-RENEWABLE RESOURCES

The principle of sustainability is based on the fact that resources are either renewable or non-renewable. Renewable resources are those that can regrow or that are always available. They include living things such as plants and animals, but also include the wind and the sun as possible energy sources. Non-renewable resources are those that have never been alive, such as minerals in the earth. They also include fossil fuels, such as coal, oil and gas, which were once living things. Coal is formed from plant material, and oil from microscopic sea animals, but because they have been formed over millions of years they are thought of as non-renewable.

future. They do not exploit a resource too quickly just for the sake of money.

A renewable resource such as a forest can be replanted. But when people cut down forests on a vast scale the soil is damaged, and the delicate balance of living things in the forest is upset.

▲ Recycling these crushed cans will save energy and money.

To avoid this people must replace the trees they cut down. If at the same time they take fruit or products such as rubber from other trees in the forest, they can preserve the forest as a resource and sustain their environment.

When we recycle aluminum cans, we reuse non-renewable resources such as bauxite, a raw material found in aluminum. This can be used again without using up new reserves, saving both energy and money.

WORLD RESOURCES

This book is about the way in which resources throughout the world have been endangered either deliberately, by accident, or more often because immediate needs have prevented people thinking ahead and planning for the future. The information is organized into six main topics and an introduction to each is given below.

ENERGY

Different countries use different amounts of energy. In the United States the amount of energy used to produce junk mail that is thrown away each day could satisfy the energy needed by 10 million people in the **developing world**. North Americans use more energy than anyone else in the world. In Canada each person uses the equivalent of 9.9 tons of coal, or 45 barrels of oil, a year. Americans use slightly less than this. People in countries such as India and Nicaragua use an average of one barrel of oil per person per year.

At present, different countries produce energy, usually in the form of electricity, in different ways: France, Belgium and South Korea use nuclear power; Canada, Norway and many countries in South America and Africa use **hydropower**, while Denmark is

▲ Drilling for oil in a Kuwaiti oil field.

investing in wind power. Many developing countries do not have their own power sources, so have to burn wood and waste plant material as fuel. These are materials that could be used to fertilize the soil for growing food.

Every type of energy has its environmental problems. Gasoline fumes cause air pollution. Nuclear energy creates long-term problems because of the radioactive waste the nuclear process creates. As fossil fuel supplies of oil and coal are used up, people need to consider alternative energy sources and find ways of using less energy, for example, by insulating their houses. Alternative energy sources are less damaging to the environment, but a wind farm of hundreds of wind turbines can look very ugly.

WATER

Water is an essential resource, but only 3 percent of the water on Earth is fresh; the rest is salt and is found in the world's oceans. Without the **water cycle** – the continuous natural recycling of water – rivers and lakes would soon dry up. People use water for industry and for irrigating crops. If they use too much water for growing crops, they lower the **water table**,

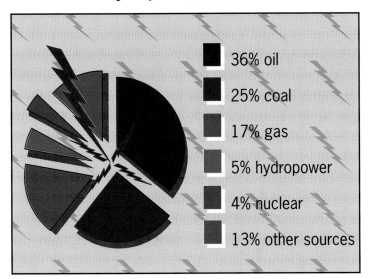

■	36% oil
■	25% coal
■	17% gas
□	5% hydropower
■	4% nuclear
■	13% other sources

▲ The figures show where the world's energy came from in 1990.

▲ *Drawing water from the village well in Burkina Faso in West Africa.*

which causes environmental problems and water shortages. Water is an especially precious resource in countries with very little rainfall. Desert countries such as Libya depend on water in natural underground reservoirs, called aquifers. These sources of water are left over from thousands of years before the region was a desert and will eventually be used up.

Although it is a precious resource, water is treated with very little respect. People pollute it with everything from sewage to highly poisonous chemicals. All over the world, rivers, seas and oceans carry the wastes of human activity.

AIR

The air we breathe is made up of gases including nitrogen, carbon dioxide and oxygen. Oxygen is the most important of these. People pollute the air with dangerous chemicals all the time. They may be immediately harmful, or dangerous over a long period.

The balance of these gases is affected by two important natural cycles, the nitrogen cycle and the carbon cycle. In the nitrogen cycle, nitrogen gas is changed into nitrates. These are chemicals that help plants grow. The gas carbon dioxide exists only in tiny amounts, but the chemical carbon is found in all living things. When anything dies the carbon is

returned either into the ground or back into the air as a gas. Carbon dioxide is known as a greenhouse gas because it traps the heat of the sun reflected off the Earth's surface.

Before the Industrial Revolution the amount of carbon dioxide in the atmosphere didn't change much. Since the Industrial Revolution more carbon dioxide has been released into the atmosphere from burning fossil fuels such as coal and oil, and also wood. The extra carbon dioxide has increased the temperature of the Earth's atmosphere. This is called global warming. No one knows what the result of this will be. The way humans use resources such as coal and oil, and the way in which they cut down and burn forests, has a direct effect on the surrounding air, the whole atmosphere and the world's climate.

SOIL

Soil is made over hundreds of years from weathered rock particles and decayed plants and animals. But it can take only a few years to lose it through bad management. Soil is part of a system that recycles the materials needed to support plants and animals and enables people to grow food. All agriculture is dependent on this natural resource and its careful management.

If people cut down too many trees, wind and rain erode the soil and wash it into the sea. Fertilizers and pesticides can poison the soil and undermine its structure, making it unsuitable for future crops. In some regions people burn natural fertilizers, such as crop remains and animal dung, as fuel, and so reduce the soil's fertility.

But people have found various successful ways of using the soil. They have built terraces on steep hillsides and used methods of watering in paddy fields that release nutrients trapped deep in the soil. As long as the soil is managed well it can sustain vast numbers of people.

MINERALS

These are the raw materials needed to supply industry. They are a non-renewable resource and have only a limited life. People are becoming more aware of the need to conserve such resources and to find ways of reusing them. Today there are schemes

▲ *Potato and rice terraces in the Philippines prevent soil erosion on the steep hillsides.*

▲ *Flowers are part of Earth's biodiversity.*

of oil are being made all the time, but despite this some experts think that the world may run out of oil by the year 2050.

BIODIVERSITY

Biodiversity describes the huge variety of living things on Earth. It is a resource made up of all plants and animals and their **genetic material**, as well as the **ecosystems** of which they are part. The Earth's biodiversity includes crops and forests. It provides, especially in developing countries, building materials from wood, and fuel from plant material and animal waste. Recently scientists have found ways of using genes from plants and animals for medical purposes. They have developed drugs and medicines. But most of this natural diversity is lost as people destroy whole habitats and ecosystems. Tropical forests, which hold up to 50 percent of all species on only 7 percent of the Earth's surface, are especially at risk.

THE FUTURE

The destruction of natural habitats reduces the chances of survival for the human race. A sensible approach to the exploitation of the Earth's natural resources will provide a safer future. This approach involves conservation and recycling, as well as looking at the resources available and managing them in a sustainable way.

for recycling glass, metals such as aluminum cans, and even plastic, which comes from oil. Less energy is used to make a new can from recycled material than from original resources.

Fossil fuels are among the most valued resources, especially the mineral resource, oil. New discoveries

▲ *The mineral iron ore is smelted in a furnace to make pig iron.*

There are many resources in the world. Six main resource categories are used in this atlas. You will find a full description of each on pages 7 to 10 of the introduction. They are represented by six key symbols, which you will find at the beginning of each entry in the book. Each example has at least one of these symbols and an additional symbol from the list below. They are also used on the maps to show where in the world the resource problem exists. Most of the examples show how people have mismanaged the world's resources, but for every problem there are often solutions that allow people to manage resources well. Such solutions come from understanding both the natural environment and the needs of people throughout the world.

The following symbols represent the six key categories of energy, soil, air, minerals, water and biodiversity. The last includes plants, animals and the natural habitats they occupy.

 ENERGY

 SOIL

 AIR

 MINERALS

 WATER

 BIODIVERSITY

 HABITAT DESTRUCTION All natural environments, from tropical forests to small ponds, can be changed or destroyed by humans. Draining wetlands, cutting down trees and building roads all destroy habitats.

FISHING AND HUNTING People exploit the natural supply of fish in seas and rivers. Where there is no careful management, overfishing can destroy this natural resource.

 AGRICULTURE People control what they grow, often by changing the environment. Wild animals have been domesticated and wild plants cultivated for use by humans.

 POLLUTION Man-made materials, such as plastics or toxic chemicals, often put the environment at risk. Too much of a natural product, such as sewage, can also be harmful.

EROSION Parts of the landscape can be worn away when people change how the land is used. When they cut down trees to farm the land, the soil is often eroded by wind or water.

 IRRIGATION Water is moved from one place to another to water crops. Badly managed irrigation can harm the soil.

ALTERNATIVE ENERGY People can use natural, renewable sources of energy, such as the sun, wind, tides and water.

RECYCLING This process allows natural and other materials to be reused. People recycle manufactured materials, such as paper and cars, so that the raw materials from which they are made can be used again.

 NON-RENEWABLE ENERGY RESOURCE These include all the fossil fuels, such as coal, gas and oil. Once they are used they cannot be replaced.

 WASTE Every process of manufacturing and most activities in the developed world create waste. It includes not only the natural resources, such as minerals used in manufacturing, but also the waste of energy resources. Waste costs money, so people are trying to find ways to create less waste.

 NUCLEAR ENERGY This is the process that releases energy from an atom of uranium. Nuclear power stations contribute to energy production, and many nations rely heavily on it as a source of energy.

 SPECIES DESTRUCTION Hunting or changing a natural habitat may destroy a species of plant or animal, some of which may not yet have been discovered by people.

 MEDICAL BENEFIT The world's natural resources, such as plants and animals, can be used in drugs to help cure diseases.

 BIOLOGICAL CONTROL Animals or insects are sometimes brought into a new habitat to control the numbers of other animals or insects living there, particularly if they are destroying crops or livestock.

 CONSERVATION Some governments and organizations help to look after natural habitats and protect the animals and plants that live and grow there.

OTHER FEATURES OF THIS ATLAS

Each large map uses different colors to show types of landscape and symbols to give you more information about a place:

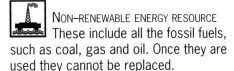

Mountain

Game reserve

Forest and scrub

National park

Desert

Capital city

Arable land

Important town or city

Frozen desert (snow, ice)

Mountain peak

Each large map has various other features. There is a small locator map, showing where in the world a particular area is. There is also a compass, which tells you where an area is in relation to north, south, east and west. A small ruler tells you the scale of the map – that is, how many kilometers (or miles) one centimeter (or inch) across the map equals. Also, the large maps have lines of latitude and longitude. These are imaginary lines, used to divide the world up into small areas, and they are measured in degrees.

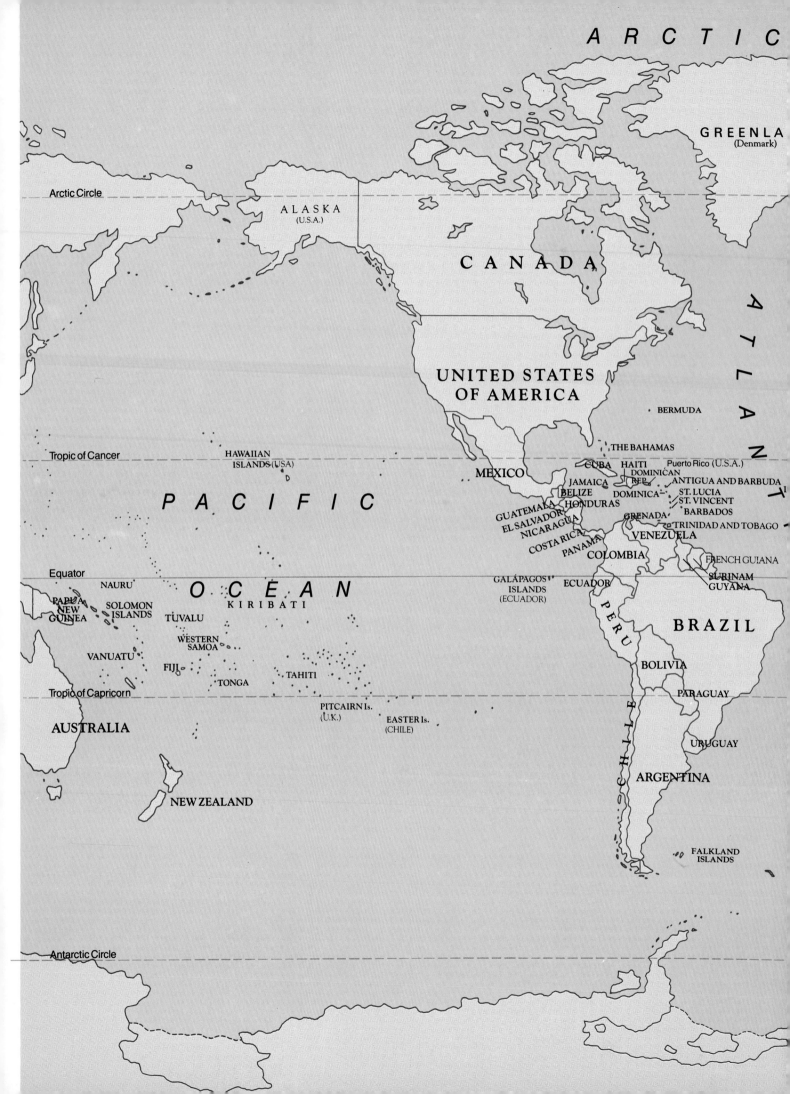

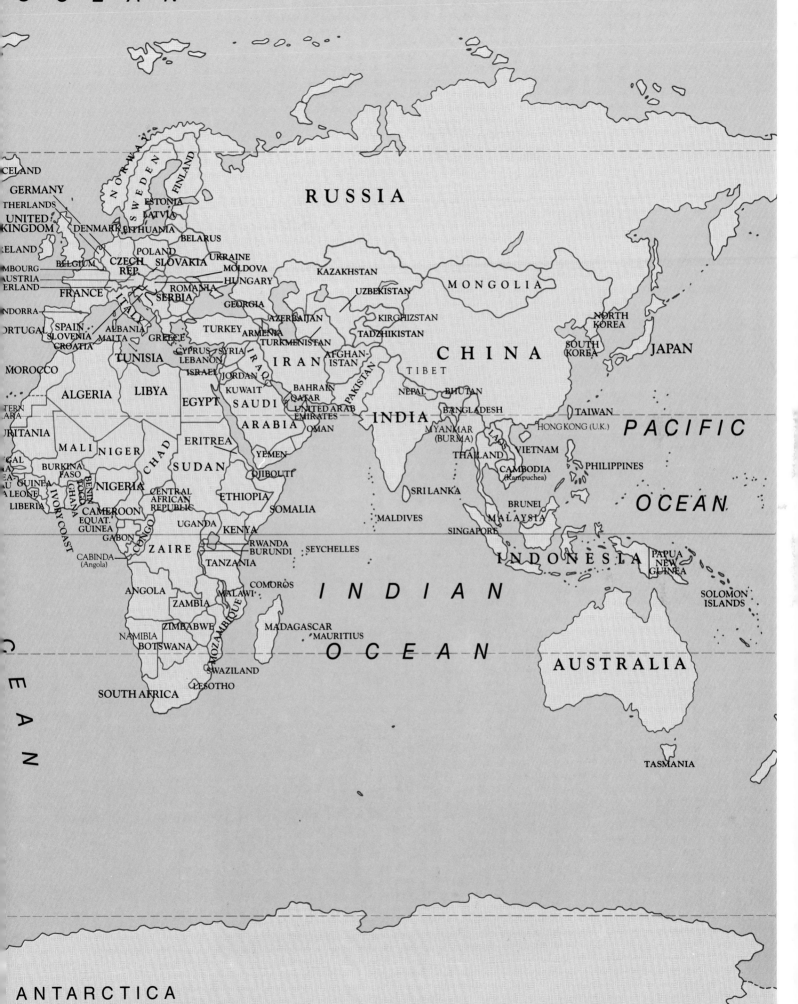

South America's greatest resource is its tropical forest, which is fed by the water from the Andes mountain chain running down the west of the region. The water spreads across the continent and spills into the ocean in the east. But the forest is being exploited rather than managed in a sustainable way. The trees are turned into woodchips or burned and the land is converted to farm or grazing land. In this way, Latin America has lost 37 percent of its tropical rain forest.

▲ TREELESS FORESTS

The destruction of the rain forest, one of the Earth's unique resources, is also destroying the delicate tropical soils and turning the region into wasteland. A heavy storm can wash away 203.5 tons of topsoil from 2.5 treeless acres. The sun then bakes the soil hard so that plants cannot grow in it. The leaves on trees turn carbon dioxide into oxygen. Cutting them down increases global warming.

▼ FISHLESS WATERS

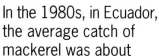

In the 1980s, in Ecuador, the average catch of mackerel was about

440,000 tons each year. Ten years later this major industry had been ruined by a combination of bad weather and overfishing.

First came strong winds that swept the young fish out to sea, away from their near-land nursery areas. This meant that a whole generation of fish was lost. The fishing boats continued to catch the adult fish, leaving too few to breed. Because of this the fish changed their behavior and gathered in groups, which made them easier to catch. Today too few fish remain to support the fishing industry, and it no longer exists.

▲ SWEET FUEL

Sugar cane has always been an important crop in South America. But when other countries began to grow sugar beet, the demand for sugar cane around the world fell.

In Brazil people found another use for it. They fermented the sugar cane and turned it into ethanol alcohol. This can be used as a fuel to drive cars and other vehicles. Almost a third of all Brazil's cars run on pure ethanol. This makes money for the cane growers, but the land might be better used for growing food.

80°

CARIBBEAN SEA

Barranquilla
Cartagena

PANAMA

70°

Maracaibo   **Caracas**
            Barquisimeto   Ciudad Guayana
                    Orinoco
            VENEZUELA   **Georgetown**
Cúcuta   **Paramaribo**
Bucaramanga   Angel Falls   GUYANA
Medellín   SURINAM   **Cayenne**
                    Mt Roraima   FRENCH
Bogotá   (9,094 ft/2,772 m)   GUIANA
COLOMBIA   Guyana Highlands

Buenaventura
Cali
Pasto

60°

50°

40°

10°

PANAMA

Esmeraldas
Quito   Mt Cotopaxi (19,344 ft/5,896 m)
ECUADOR   Mt Chimborazo
Guayaquil   (20,561 ft/6,272 m)
Cuenca   Iquitos   Leticia
                Fonte Boa

Chiclayo
Trujillo
Mt Huascarán
(22,205 ft/6,768 m)
Callao
Lima   **Manu National Park**
              Cuzco
Arequipa   Lake
              Titicaca
Puno   **La Paz**
              Cochabamba
Iquique   Santa Cruz
              Sucre
              Potosí

Antofagasta
Salta

Copiapó
San Miguel
de Tucumán
Córdoba

Valparaíso
Santiago   San Luis
River Bío-Bío   **Buenos Aires**
Concepción   **ARGENTINA**
Temuco   Pampas

Puerto Montt   Colorado
                Bahía Blanca

Patagonia

GULF OF
SAN JORGE
Comodoro
Rivadavia

Punta Arenas
Tierra Del
Fuego
Cape Horn

Negro

Manaus   Amazon
            Madeira
Selvas

Rio Branco
Cobija
BOLIVIA

B R   A   Z   I   L

Macapa

Belém

Fortaleza

Natal

Recife

Maceió

Salvador

Porto Velho

Cuiaba   Mato
              Grosso

PARAGUAY
Asunción   Coronel
              Oviedo

Gran Chaco

Salado

Paraguay

Campo
Grande

Londrina   Campinas
                          Niterói
Uberlandia   Rio de Janeiro
              Brasília   São Paulo
              Goiânia   Montes Claros
BRAZILIAN
HIGHLANDS

Curitiba

São Francisco

Campos

Tocantins

Xingú

Paraná
Uruguay   Uruguaiana
              Salto   Porto Alegre
              Paysandú
Rosario   URUGUAY   Rio Grande
              Montevideo
La Plata

Mar del Plata

PACIFIC
OCEAN

ATLANTIC
OCEAN

Tropic of Capricorn

Equator   0°

10°

20°

30°

40°

50°

N
W   E
S

0   500   1000   1500   2000   2500 km
cm   1   2   3   4   5   6   7   8   9   10
inches   1   2   3   4
0   500   1000   1500 miles

Falkland Islands
(Islas Malvinas)
(United Kingdom)

100°   90°   80°   70°   60°   50°   40°   30°   20°

CENTRAL AMERICA AND THE CARIBBEAN

This region is covered in lush tropical forest, but much of the forest is being cut down to grow cash crops, such as coffee, sugar, bananas and other fruit. These crops are sold on the world market. The very fast growth in population means that many of the region's natural resources are being used up, and more and more people migrate from the countryside into the cities. Mexico City is one of the fastest-growing cities in the world. Many of the Caribbean islands have a tourist industry that is also changing the region's natural environment.

MANGROVES ▶

Much of the coast in this region is covered by mangrove swamps, which are a valuable resource. They provide an important natural habitat for over 2,000 species of plants and fish, including many commercial fish species. Over the years people have used these areas in a sustainable way for supplies of wood for fuel and charcoal. Mangrove swamps also help to protect the coastline from erosion. But many countries see mangroves as wasteland. They are especially under threat in Jamaica, Haiti, the Dominican Republic, Puerto Rico, and Trinidad and Tobago. These habitats are disappearing for many reasons. Land is being reclaimed for tourist use, such as building hotels. People are taking wood to produce chipboard, and the habitat is being changed for agriculture and shrimp farming.

GREEN REVOLUTION

In the 1960s, plant breeders at the International Maize and Wheat Improvement Centre bred new, experimental strains of rice, wheat and maize. These produced larger crops than before from the same amount of land. From 1944 to 1967 Mexico's maize crops doubled and its rice crops trebled. This "green revolution" worked well at first, but successful crops needed large quantities of chemical fertilizers and pesticides.

Today some grain crops have become less pest resistant as a result. Many countries cannot afford to buy the chemicals they need to produce high yields and protect the crops from disease and pests.

▼ GOING BANANAS

The main crop grown on St. Lucia is bananas. But as the tourist industry began to grow in the Caribbean, many of the banana workers left to join the new industry. This meant there were fewer people to work in the plantations. The banana plantations were nearly ruined through neglect, which would have damaged the country's economy and environment. People are a resource, and where they work is important.

16

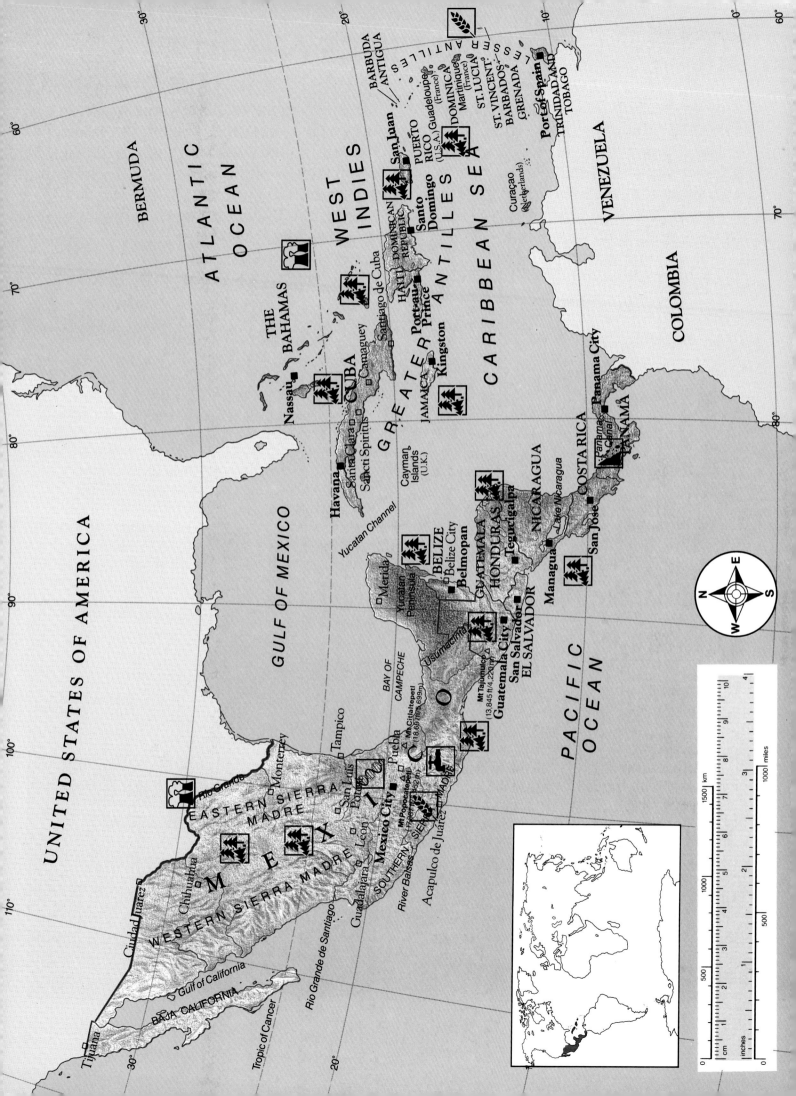

UNITED STATES OF AMERICA

The United States has many natural resources that have been rapidly exploited in a relatively short time. It is heavily industrialized and has an agricultural system so productive that it provides food for many other countries around the world. The country's rapid growth and development has meant that its natural resources have been heavily exploited. Today the United States, like other developed countries, suffers from pollution, the destruction of natural habitats and the bad management of many of its resources.

CROPLAND
- USA
- Rest of the world

CROPS
- Wheat
- Oats
- Sorghum
- Maize

▼ SUMMITVILLE

Summitville is a gold mine high in the Rocky Mountains in Colorado, where cyanide and other heavy metals are used to extract gold from the soil. These metals were being washed into the Alamosa River, which provides water for farms and ranches before flowing into the Rio Grande River.

Within a year of the mine being opened, fish began to die in a reservoir 24 km (15 mi) downstream and irrigation equipment was corroded. The private company operating the mine could not control the pollution, and the mine was taken over by the Environmental Protection Agency in 1993. The cost to the government of trying to save the environment will be enormous.

▲ AGRICULTURE

Providing food is the United States' biggest business. But for every 100 people living there, only two are involved in producing food for the nation and for the rest of the world. Until 100 years ago most people worked on the land, growing food. Today that human energy has been replaced by technology and the energy that drives it. American farmers use only 11 percent of the world's cropland to grow 15 percent of the world's wheat, 21 percent of the world's oats, 36 percent of sorghum and 46 percent of maize (see above). But providing such vast quantities of food has a cost. Burning fossil fuel to drive farm machinery creates pollution. Pesticides are sprayed on the crops and fertilizers are used. These pollute the environment. The amount of crops the soil can grow is pushed to its limits and 5.5 billion tons of soil are lost each year. Nobody knows how long the soil can continue to be exploited in this way.

▼ IRRIGATION

Irrigation puts a heavy demand on natural water resources. It is often used in dry regions where there is a great deal of land but little readily available water all year round. The Ogallala Aquifer runs underground from southern Dakota to northwestern Texas and contains ground water that cannot easily be replaced. Water is pumped out of the aquifer to irrigate the Texas plains, where nearly 40 percent of the US grain-fed beef cattle are raised. As a result, 70 percent of the water in the aquifer has been lost.

▲ DUST BOWLS

In the 1930s, because of intensive farming, much of the United States' topsoil in the Midwest was eroded and blown away. Now a new way of reducing soil loss is being used by American farmers. They plough less and leave a third of the field's leftover plant material to hold together and fertilize the soil. This is called conservation tillage. But more than a quarter of US cropland is still being eroded very fast. The worst affected areas are the Central Valley of California, the **watersheds** of the Mississippi and Missouri rivers and the hill farms of Washington State.

ALTERNATIVE ENERGY

The United States has very varied weather, which can be used effectively to supply alternative energy. By the end of 1987, wind farms in San Gorgonio, Tehachapi and Altamont Pass, California, were producing 1,437 megawatts of electricity from nearly 17,000 turbines. This provides 15 percent of San Francisco's electricity. In other places, such as Idaho, the sun can be used to provide electricity to farms and homes via sun, or solar, collectors. In the United States this alternative form of energy generation supplied more than 100,000 homes in the early 1990s compared with fewer than 1,000 homes in the 1970s.

WATER POLLUTION

In 1992 the Environmental Protection Agency surveyed one-third of the rivers in the United States and found that at least half were too polluted to use for recreation, drinking water and fish farming. Over half the pollution was caused by chemicals in the soil from pesticides and fertilizers being washed into the rivers. In the Snake and Columbia rivers, 200 species of fish are in danger of dying out. In 1991, 2,000 beaches and a third of the country's shellfish waters were closed because of pollution from untreated sewage.

AIR POLLUTION ▶

In developed countries, legislation is an effective way of changing people's attitude towards their environment. Some cities in the USA are well known for their smogs. In hot weather the chemicals in polluted air react with sunlight to make ozone. When there are very high levels of ozone, pollution warnings are given, called advisories. In the summer of 1988 Philadelphia had 23 advisories, New York City 21 and Washington 12. This dropped to half the number of advisories in the summer of 1993. From 1982 to 1992 the pollution from carbon monoxide was down by 30 per cent, from sulphur dioxide down by 20 per cent and from lead down by 89 per cent. The 1990 Clean Air Act has helped to improve the quality of the air in the USA.

RECYCLING

In the US about 70 percent of people recycle much of their household waste. In 1991, 62 percent of the nation's aluminum drink cans were recycled. Recycled aluminum cans use 95 percent less energy to produce than new ones. New cans also use up new supplies of metal. Seattle was one of the first cities to introduce recycling. In recent years people living there have begun to throw away less solid waste. But the problem remains —because the amount of rubbish the nation produces has risen from 1.2 kg (2.64 lb) per person per day in 1960 to 1.9 kg (4.18 lb) in 1990.

MONOCULTURE MADNESS

Intensive farming is a modern method of agriculture where farmers grow a large amount of just a few crops, or even just one crop (a monoculture). This is done to produce food that can be sold relatively cheaply to a mass market. When land is intensively farmed in this way, vast fields are planted with a single crop, such as wheat. Such a large amount of one kind of food attracts pests, so farmers have to use chemical pesticides to kill them. After each spraying a few of the pests survive to breed new pests, which are not affected by the pesticide. So more and different pesticides are needed to control the next generation of pests. This kind of farming eventually causes serious environmental pollution.

Canada is a country rich in natural resources. There are softwood forests, which provide wood for building and for making paper, and in the south there are vast prairies, where farmers grow wheat and grain to sell to the world. There are also large areas of mountains, rivers and lakes where hydroelectricity schemes have been set up to provide an alternative source of energy.

DAMS AND CHANGE ▶

Hydroelectricity is an important development. It is usually less harmful to the environment than traditional ways of making energy. But some large, high-tech dam-building schemes can create major changes in the natural environment.

A dam-building program in Quebec, called the La Grande Development, has had some serious ecological side effects. As the reservoir filled with water, the remains of dead plants began to build up. Bacteria formed to break down the plant remains, but these also changed mercury in the rocks into methyl mercury and released it into the water. The fish in the reservoir absorbed high levels of mercury – as high as 100 million times greater than the surrounding water. The mercury in the fish then poisoned the people who caught and ate them.

ACID RAIN

Acid rain pollutes about 700,000 lakes in Canada. Sulfur dioxide from industrial smoke in the United States blows north into Canada and reacts with water to form a weak acid that falls as acid rain. As the water in the lakes becomes more acid, fish cannot use their gills to breathe and eventually they suffocate. Over time the acid kills most living things in the lake.

In addition acid rain weakens trees in forest areas, especially pine and fir trees. The acidity makes the trees more vulnerable to disease.

▼ PRAIRIES AND PESTICIDES

Enough wheat is grown on Canada's prairies to supply the rest of the world with the wheat it

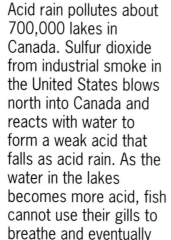

needs to make bread each day. Farming methods are intensive and farmers use large amounts of fertilizers and pesticides. They also use huge combine harvesters to collect the crops. Where there is intensive farming there is a danger that too many chemicals will eventually damage the rich soil. If the land is to continue to produce crops for the world, farmers must manage the land in a sustainable way. But even where farmers could farm organically, using only natural fertilizers and no pesticides, they would at first lose money from smaller crops. Solutions often have too high an immediate price.

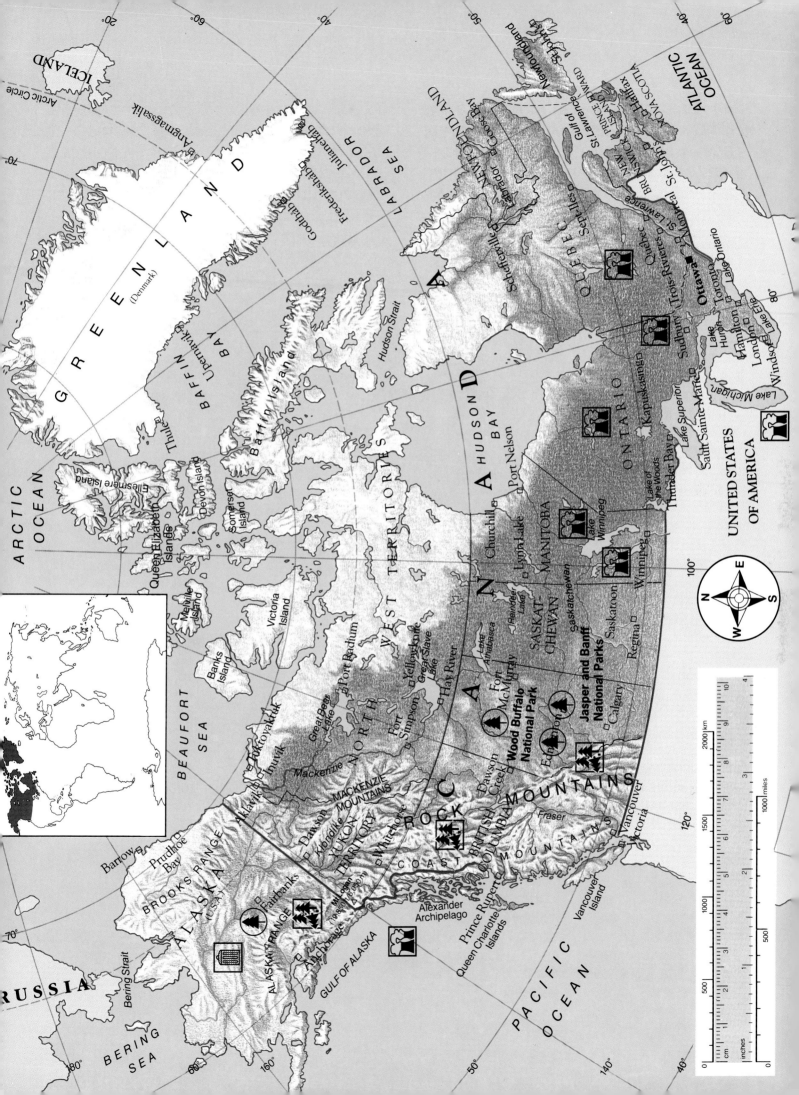

ICELAND

Arctic Circle

Angmagssalik

G R E E N L A N D
(Denmark)

Upernavik
Umanak
Godhavn
Frederikshåb
Julianehåb
Thule

ARCTIC OCEAN

RUSSIA

Bering Strait

BERING SEA

Barrow

Prudhoe Bay

BEAUFORT SEA

BROOKS RANGE

ALASKA (U.S.A.)

Fairbanks

Mt. McKinley (1980) (6,194 m)

ALASKA RANGE

Anchorage

GULF OF ALASKA

BAFFIN BAY

Queen Elizabeth Islands

Ellesmere Island

Devon Island

Melville Island

Banks Island

Victoria Island

Somerset Island

Baffin Island

Hudson Strait

WEST TERRITORIES

NORTH

Aklavik
Tuktoyaktuk
Inuvik

Great Bear Lake

Port Radium

MACKENZIE MOUNTAINS

Fort Simpson

Great Slave Lake

Yellowknife

Hay River

Mackenzie

YUKON TERRITORY

Dawson
Klondike

Whitehorse

COAST

ROCK

MOUNTAINS

Dawson Creek

BRITISH COLUMBIA

Fraser

Prince Rupert

Queen Charlotte Islands

Alexander Archipelago

Vancouver Island

Victoria

Vancouver

PACIFIC OCEAN

LABRADOR SEA

HUDSON BAY

Churchill

Port Nelson

Lynn Lake

Reindeer Lake

Lake Athabasca

Fort McMurray

Wood Buffalo National Park

Jasper and Banff National Parks

Edmonton

MOUNTAINS

Calgary

SASKAT-CHEWAN

Saskatchewan

Saskatoon

Regina

MANITOBA

Lake Winnipeg

Winnipeg

Lake of the Woods

Thunder Bay

Lake Superior

Sault Sainte Marie

C A N A D A

Scheffervillle

Labrador

Goose Bay

NEWFOUNDLAND

Gulf of St. Lawrence

St. John's

PRINCE EDWARD ISLAND

NOVA SCOTIA

Halifax

NEW BRUNSWICK

Saint John

St. Lawrence

Sept-Îles

Trois-Rivières
Québec
Montréal

QUEBEC

ONTARIO

Kapuskasing

Sudbury

Ottawa

Lake Ontario

Toronto

Hamilton

Lake Erie

London

Windsor

Lake Huron

Lake Michigan

ATLANTIC OCEAN

UNITED STATES OF AMERICA

N
W   E
S

2000 km
1500
1000
500
0

1000 miles
500
0

cm
inches

Scandinavia's softwood forests are one of the region's major natural resources. They supply the world with wood for pulp, used in paper making, and pine, for building. The sea is another major source of food and income for the people. Scandinavia's main sources of energy are oil and gas under the North Sea. The region's mountains and rivers are also a natural resource for hydroelectricity. Large areas of Scandinavia have been affected by the acid rain created by industrial countries to the south.

HOT ROCKS ▶

Iceland has an unusual energy source called geothermal energy. This is a natural heat energy that occurs in some parts of the world where the rock structure is right, in particular Iceland and New Zealand. Water from deep under the ground is heated up naturally and forced to the surface as a geyser. A geyser is a natural spring that gives off steam and hot water. Geothermal heat provides a natural central-heating system. In Iceland it supplies all the energy needs of the capital city, Reykjavik. As well as hot water and heating for people's homes, it is also used to heat greenhouses and for industrial purposes. Geothermal energy is an important alternative energy source, but it is available only in some parts of the world. Until recently it has been used only on a small scale.

ENERGY RICH

Norway has exploited the rich supplies of oil and natural gas under the North Sea. But because these are non-renewable resources they will eventually run out. Denmark has decided to use less oil and to stop using nuclear power. It has invested in energy resources such as wind and has 1,400 windmills linking into a **national grid**. Scandinavia also has the resources to develop wave and tidal power. These renewable energy resources will help reduce pollution.

▼ FUTURE FISH?

The seas around Scandinavia have always been an important source of food. Iceland, Norway and Denmark each catch more than 1.1 million tons of fish every year. But problems have been caused by fishing boats that use nets with small holes. These are too small for the young fish to swim through and so leave fewer and fewer fish to breed. Over the years the numbers of fish drop and the fishing industry suffers.

The Economic Exclusion Zone, established in 1983, was a successful attempt to deal with this problem. It gave each nation control of waters within 320 km (200 mi) of its coast, so that they can manage their fishing more carefully.

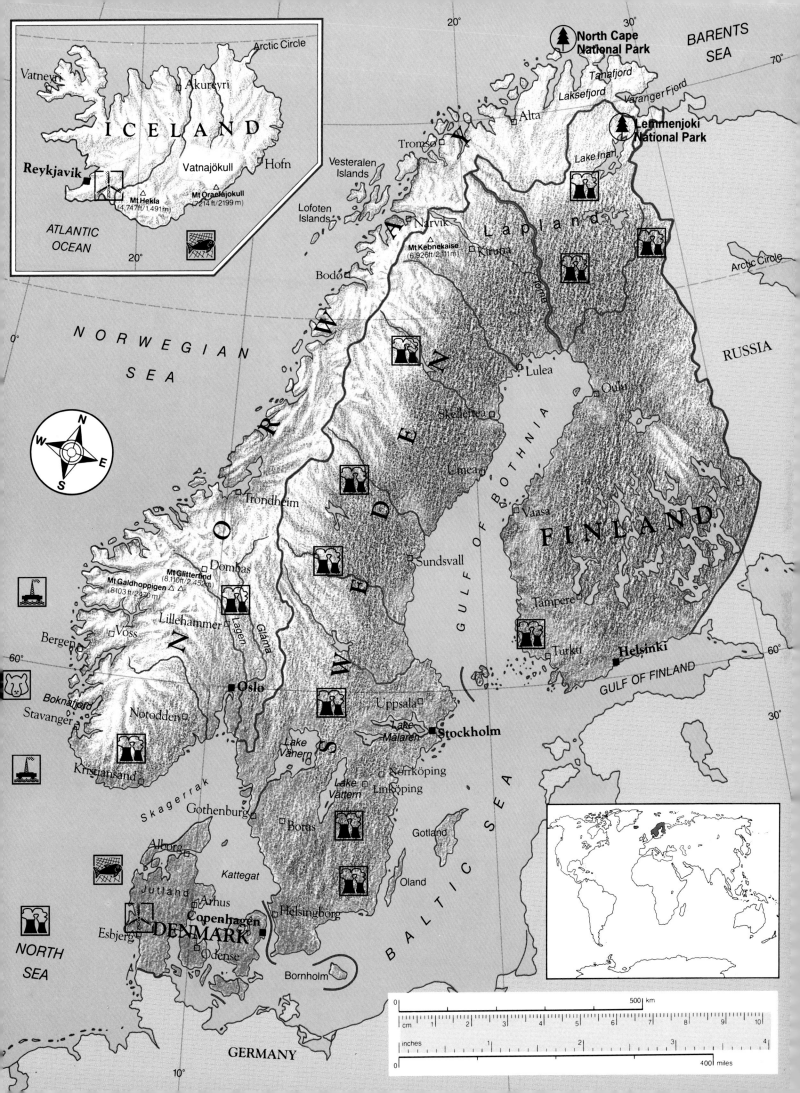

ICELAND

Reykjavik

Vatnajökull

Hofn

Mt Hekla
(4,747ft/1,491m)

Mt Oraefajökull
(7214 ft/2199 m)

Akureyri

Vatneyri

ATLANTIC
OCEAN

Arctic Circle

20°

20°

North Cape
National Park

BARENTS
SEA

Tanafjord

Laksefjord

Varanger Fjord

70°

Alta

Lemmenjoki
National Park

Tromsø

Lake Inari

Lapland

Arctic Circle

RUSSIA

Vesterålen
Islands

Narvik

Mt Kebnekaise
(6,926ft/2,111m)

Kiruna

Lofoten
Islands

Bodø

Torne

NORWEGIAN
SEA

N
O
R
W
A
Y

S
W
E
D
E
N

Luleå

Oulu

0°

Skellefteå

GULF OF BOTHNIA

Umeå

Trondheim

Vaasa

FINLAND

Dombås

Mt Glittertind
(8,110ft/2,452m)

Mt Galdhøppigen
(8103 ft/2470 m)

Sundsvall

Lillehammer

Lågen

Glama

Bergen

Voss

Tampere

Mt Kebnekaise

60°

Notodden

Oslo

Turku

Helsinki

60°

GULF OF FINLAND

30°

Uppsala

Boknafjord

Stavanger

Lake
Mälaren

Stockholm

Kristiansand

Norrköping

Lake
Vänern

Linköping

Lake
Vättern

Skagerrak

Gothenburg

Borås

Gotland

Ålborg

Kattegat

Öland

Jutland

Århus

Helsingborg

Copenhagen

DENMARK

B
A
L
T
I
C

S
E
A

NORTH
SEA

Esbjerg

Odense

Bornholm

GERMANY

10°

20°

30°

0   500 km

cm 1 2 3 4 5 6 7 8 9 10

inches   1   2   3   4

0   400 miles

West Europe was the first region to change from a rural and agricultural way of life to an industrial and manufacturing one, producing goods to be sold around the world. This change began around the mid-18th century and created many environmental problems, including pollution. By the end of the 1700s Britain had destroyed most of its forests and had begun to exploit coal as a fuel instead of wood. People began to use iron ores to make steel for building. The rest of Europe followed and began to exploit its own resources of coal and other raw materials.

▼ HEDGEROWS

In the 1970s farmers in West Europe, especially Great Britain, were given subsidies to grow wheat. Miles of hedgerows were cut down to make bigger fields for the wheat and to make it easier to harvest with large combine harvesters.

The change from a traditional to a more open landscape destroyed wildlife habitats and allowed wind and rain to cause soil erosion. Huge stores of unwanted wheat were gathered.

Twenty years later, the subsidies have stopped and some farmers are being paid to replant their hedgerows.

▲ RIVER RHINE

In the 1970s the Rhine was one of the most polluted rivers in the world. It passed through many industrialized countries and carried a heavy load of toxic chemical wastes, heavy metals and sewage.

Today it is much cleaner and there are fish in some parts of the river. But it is still heavily polluted by salt, which is washed out from agricultural land and mining operations. Much of the salt comes from the potash mines in the Alsace region of France. By the time the Rhine reaches the Netherlands, the high levels of salt make the land around the river unsuitable for growing crops.

Faeroe Islands (Denmark)

Shetland Islands

Orkney Islands

NORWAY

60°

DENMARK

FINLAND

60°

NORTH SEA

Ben Nevis (4,406 ft / 1,343 m)

SCOTLAND

Glasgow   Edinburgh

UNITED KINGDOM

NORTHERN IRELAND   Belfast

Galway

IRELAND   Dublin   Liverpool   Manchester

Cork   IRISH SEA   WALES

1   2

London

Dover   Bruges

Calais

Plymouth   ENGLISH CHANNEL   Lille   Brussels   Liège   Cologne

1 Snowdonia National Park

2 Peak District National Park

3 Lake District National Park

Channel Islands (U.K.)

ATLANTIC OCEAN

BAY OF BISCAY

Nantes

FRANCE

CENTRAL MASSIF

Bordeaux   Dordogne

Garonne

CANTABRIAN MOUNTAINS   Bilbao

PORTUGAL

Porto   Duero

SPAIN

Tagus   Madrid

Guadiana

Cordoba

Seville   Guadalquivir

Mt Mulhacen (11,411 ft / 3,478 m)

Lisbon

Málaga

Gibraltar (United Kingdom)

Coto Donana Reserve

MOROCCO

Kiel   Rostock

Hamburg   Elbe   Oder   POLAND

NETHERLANDS   Berlin

Amsterdam   Utrecht   Hanover   Leipzig   Dresden

The Hague   IJsselmeer   Weimar   Jena

BELGIUM   Bonn   Frankfurt   Main   Bavarian Forest National Park

LUXEMBOURG   Mannheim   CZECH REPUBLIC

Luxembourg   GERMANY   SLOVAKIA

Strasbourg   Rhine   Munich   Salzburg   Vienna

Paris   Vosges   Zurich   AUSTRIA   Graz   HUNGARY

Dijon   Basle   Innsbruck   Mt Grossglockner (12,457 ft / 3,797 m)

Berne   SWITZERLAND   ALPS   SLOVENIA   Trieste   CROATIA

Lausanne   Verona   Venice

Mont Blanc (15,771 ft / 4,807 m)   Milan   Po   Bologna   SAN MARINO

Lyon   Turin   ADRIATIC SEA

Genoa   APENNINES   ITALY

Avignon   MONACO   Florence

Toulouse   Marseille   Tiber   Abruzzo National Park

Pico de Aneto (11,168 ft / 3,404 m)   Camargue Regional Park   Rome   Bari

PYRENEES   ANDORRA   Corsica (France)   Naples

Zaragoza   Ebro   Barcelona

Majorca   Sardinia   40°

Valencia

Balearic Islands   Palermo   Messina

Marsala   Sicily   Catania

MEDITERRANEAN SEA

ALGERIA   TUNISIA   Valletta   MALTA

N
W   E
S

0   500   1000 km

cm   1   2   3   4   5   6   7   8   9   10

inches   1   2   3   4

0   500 miles

10°   0°   10°   20°

50°

20°

10°

40°

0°

TIDAL POWER

In Britain there are plans to build a large tidal barrage across the Severn estuary between Brean Down, west of Weston-super-Mare, and Lavernock point, near Cardiff in Wales. Here there is 11 meters (36.3 ft) between the low and high tidemark. This difference is important in creating the tidal energy that can be turned into electricity. At high tide the sea would fill the reservoir and be trapped by the sluicegates, which control the flow of the water. The water would then flow out over **turbines** and generate up to 7 percent of Britain's electricity.

Although hydroelectricity is an important use of resources, the planners must also think about the environment, because the area is an important wetland habitat for plants and animals.

▲ NORTH SEA

Every day waste from the industries along the major European rivers, such as the Elbe, Weser, Ems, Schelde, Rhine-Meuse, Forth, Humber, Tyne, Tees and Thames, pours into the North Sea. Boats dump industrial and sewage sludge on the sea bed; burning at sea causes toxic waste and there is further waste from shipping and offshore oil and gas industries. Each year about 1.65 tons of mercury is dumped into the Thames estuary. Large amounts of fertilizers and pesticides, 1,650,000 tons of nitrates and 110,000 tons of phosphates are all washed into the sea.

The North Sea is polluted, but a connection between pollution and the problems that are occurring cannot always be scientifically proved. At present fish, seals, birds and plant life are all affected by disease and viruses. **Algal blooms** feed on the pollution and make the problem worse. These signs show that all is not well. But whether a definite link between pollution and the problems in the North Sea can be proved scientifically remains to be seen.

BIOFUEL

Many developed countries bury their waste in the ground, transporting it to selected sites around the country. Transporting it uses energy and the waste can also cause severe pollution problems. But some of the waste is **organic** and breaks down. As it does so, it gives off natural gases, usually methane gas, which can be a source of fuel. The gas is piped out of the ground and burned in a similar way to natural gas. In Britain the use of landfill gas saves around 178,200 tons of coal each year. In Germany landfill gas saves 148,500 tons of coal each year.

THE MEDITERRANEAN

This sea is enclosed by land. Every year 473 billion tons of sewage, domestic waste, chemicals and detergents pour into the sea from the countries surrounding it, including from the many tourist resorts along the coasts. River waters from the industrialized countries pour in 5,500 tons of zinc, 1,540 tons of lead, 1,045 tons of chromium and 11 tons of mercury a year. Mediterranean plant and animal life is being poisoned, and conditions are becoming dangerous for people who live in the region and for the tourists who stay there. The countries around the Mediterranean have now agreed to try to reduce pollution and clean up the sea.

▲ HERRING FISHERY

The North Sea herring fishery was once a major industry in Britain. But in the 1900s overfishing reduced the number of fish and made it harder for fishermen to earn a living. One problem was that as the numbers of fish dropped, the catches included more and more young fish. This meant that they could not breed, and so in time the stocks grew even smaller.

Research into the reasons for the failure of the fishing industry has led to a better understanding of how to manage this resource more effectively.

▼ ALPINE ATTACK

In the Alps, remote rural communities have been replaced by hotels. Each year these are filled with the 20 million or so visitors who come to the Alps for winter sports. Bulldozers have changed the natural environment. They have removed trees, which formed a barrier against the snow, so that avalanches and flash floods have become more common. The streams and rivers have become polluted with sewage. Nearly 60 species of alpine plants have become extinct this century because of a change in their habitat. This shows how tourism, and the money it brings, can mean that not enough care is taken of the environment.

FOREST MANAGEMENT

All over Europe forests are grown to make money. **Softwood**, or conifer, forests are fast-growing, and the wood is used for many things including pulp for making paper. Replanting trees can be a good use of resources and helps to reduce carbon dioxide in the atmosphere. But where the forests are grown in plantations the regular lines of trees spoil the look of the countryside. Because the trees are planted close together there is not enough light for other plants to grow, and the natural habitat is lost. Today many countries are growing softwood and **hardwood** trees together in a less harsh and damaging way.

EAST EUROPE

In the early 1990s there were many major political changes in East Europe. Until then most countries were ruled by communist governments. These governments exploited the natural resources, but did not put enough money and research into protecting the natural environment. Over the years there has been widespread industrial pollution and a great deal of waste of energy and resources. In some countries, the effects of pollution from the production of nuclear power could harm the environment for thousands of years.

▶ ORGANIC FARMING

Farming in East Europe is still very traditional. In Poland there are 1.5 million horses, which are used on farms instead of machinery. There are many farmers in East Europe who own small farms of about 25 acres. They do not use fertilizers or pesticides, but farm organically. This means that they use natural fertilizers such as animal manure. Farmers change their crops regularly and grow different crops together. This is good for the soil and helps to avoid a build-up of pests, which tend to attack single large crops.

As chemicals and modern machinery become more available to Eastern European countries, these traditional farming methods may be replaced by modern ones, causing damage to the environment.

◀ A BETTER LIFE?

Because of political changes in East Europe, Western goods have become available to some people. This has brought problems. For example, more people now own washing machines, but rural areas cannot cope with the extra detergents washed into the rivers. In the past, because of a shortage of resources, packaging for food and drink was simple. Western packaging creates more paper, plastic and metal waste. But the countries in this region do not have the modern technology necessary to process the waste.

DENMARK

BALTIC SEA

GERMANY

10° 20° 30°

Gdańsk

Szczecin

Oder

Poznań

POLAND

Vistula

Bialowieza
National Park

Warsaw

Łódź

Wrocław

50° 50°

ORE MOUNTAINS

Prague

CZECH REPUBLIC

Ostrava

Brno

Kraków

Tatra Mountains
National Park

CARPATHIAN MOUNTAINS

SLOVAKIA

Košice

Bratislava

Miskolc

AUSTRIA

Danube

Budapest

Debrecen

HUNGARY

Lake Balaton

Hungarian Plain

Cluj

Mureş

ROMANIA

Mt Moldoveanul
(8,348ft/2,548m)

SLOVENIA

Ljubljana

Zagreb

Pécs

Szeged

Arad

Timişoara

TRANSYLVANIAN ALPS

Braşov

Rijeka

Drava

CROATIA

Sava

Belgrade

Ploieşti

Plitvice
National Park

BOSNIA

(YUGOSLAVIA)

Bucharest

Constanţa

DINARIC

HERZEGOVINA

Sarajevo

SERBIA

Danube

BLACK SEA

ADRIATIC SEA

Split

ALPS

MONTENEGRO

Dubrovnik

BALKAN MOUNTAINS

BULGARIA

Varna

ITALY

Sofia

Stara Zagora

Burgas

Plovdiv

Skopje

MACEDONIA

Tirana

ALBANIA

40° 40°

Vlorë

Korçë

Mt Olympus
(9,570ft/2,918m)

Thessaloniki

Corfu

Ionian Islands

AEGEAN SEA

Lesbos

TURKEY

PINDUS MOUNTAINS

GREECE

Chios

N
W E
S

Patrai

Corinth

Athens

Peloponnese

MEDITERRANEAN SEA

Rhodes

0 500 km

cm 1 2 3 4 5 6 7 8 9 10

inches 1 2 3 4

0 500 miles

Crete

NUCLEAR POWER

Since the end of communist rule in East Europe, the rest of the world has been concerned about its production of nuclear power. There are 25 nuclear reactors that may be particularly dangerous. In Russia, Ukraine and Lithuania there are 15 water-cooled, graphite-moderated reactors. A reactor of this type caused the major explosion at Chernobyl in 1986. In the former Czechoslovakia and in Bulgaria, the international inspectors found basic design defects in the reactors, such as no emergency cooling systems. The region needs the energy provided by the reactors, but any accident would have terrible environmental consequences.

▲ THE BLACK SEA

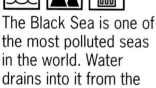

The Black Sea is one of the most polluted seas in the world. Water drains into it from the industrial and agricultural regions of nine different countries. Each year the River Danube deposits 1,100 tons of chromium, 990 tons of copper, 66 tons of mercury, 4,950 tons of lead, 6,600 tons of zinc and 55,000 tons of oil into the sea.

In the northwest areas of the sea, pollution has upset the natural balance, causing algal blooms and harming the animal life. Because of this the fishing industry has been severely affected. In the 1960s fishing boats caught 26 different species of fish – now only six species survive.

But because the Black Sea region is a heavily developed tourist area for Eastern Europe, people are beginning to demand a cleaner sea.

COPSA MICA

At Copsa Mica in Romania two factories reveal a lack of concern for the local people and their environment. One factory smelts lead, cadmium, zinc and copper; the other produces rubber tires. Each year, during the manufacturing process, 33,000 tons of chemicals pour into the air from the factory chimneys, causing acid rain in the region. In 1990, tests showed that local children had twice the safe level of lead in their blood. Babies are born sick and many people suffer from asthma. The soil is polluted with high levels of cadmium and lead. This was once the most polluted place in Central Europe. In 1993 the two factories were closed down, but the problem will continue until technology is used that will reduce pollution.

POLITICAL CONSERVATION

Until the political changes of the nineties there were areas of East Europe that formed a neutral barrier between countries in the east and the west. Now there is no longer a need for such barriers. Conservationists are planning to use these areas and existing national parks to create a series of national and multi-national nature reserves. These reserves will provide undisturbed habitats for the birds and animals of the region. So far, there are 24 national parks that may be chosen, including the Bayerische Wald National Park in Germany, and Bialowieza in Poland, as well as the Danube delta.

▲ BROWN COAL

More than half the electricity in the Czech Republic and Slovakia is generated from brown coal, which is high in sulfur. Brown coal is mined in northern Bohemia from opencut and underground pits. Opencut mining involves stripping the land's surface to reach mineral resources that lie just beneath it. Between 1989 and 1994, 112 villages were destroyed in order to mine this valuable coal. Even towns of historic interest were being demolished.

▼ DYING DOLPHINS

The tuna fishing industry along the coast of Greece and in the Adriatic has been very successful over the last 15 years. But fishing methods meant that dolphins were often trapped and drowned in the fishing nets. There was an international outcry, and people all over the world stopped buying tuna caught in this way. Many countries now fish for tuna using hooks and lines, which do not endanger the dolphins' lives.

In Northern Africa there are great rivers and mountains and desert landscapes. Some countries, such as Libya, have oil. Several others, along the Mediterranean coast, have developed tourist industries. Both tourism and oil have had an effect on the environment. In the nations south of the Sahara, people rely mainly on agriculture. But their environment has been destroyed and their whole way of life turned upside down by war and, in recent years, severe drought.

NATURAL CONTROL

In 1988 an insect called the New World screwworm fly spread over 16,000 sq mi of Libyan countryside. Female screwworm flies lay their eggs in open cuts on animals such as cattle, and the larvae eat the animals' flesh. In Libya 12,000 animals died from infection. Five North African countries were at risk of losing up to 70 million domestic livestock.

Scientists dealt with the problem by a method called biological control. Large numbers of sterile male flies were brought into the area. When they mated with the female insects the eggs weren't fertilized and the insects eventually died out. No animals have died because of the fly since 1991. Biological control keeps pests under control without harming the environment, but sometimes it can go wrong (see page 52).

▲ ARID LAND

Recently, this region has had lower than average rainfall, and there have been changes in the way land is used. This has caused environmental problems. The region, which is known as the Sahel, includes the countries Senegal, Mauritania, Mali, Burkina Faso, Niger, Chad, Sudan, Ethiopia, Somalia and Djibouti. Land that was used to grow crops for local people is now used to grow **cash crops**, such as peanuts or coffee. People have been forced to grow food crops on land that has quickly become overgrazed by domestic animals. Although the land has been irrigated, overfarming has damaged the balance of the soil. This has caused a build-up of salts in the soil, which has killed crops. Trees have been cut down for fuel, or have been eaten by animals such as goats, so that the topsoil is easily blown away. This makes it hard for people to grow enough food to eat.

▼ TOXIC WASTE

In 1987 Italy delivered 2,200 tons of chemical waste to the Nigerian town of Koko. It was dumped in 10,000 barrels in the ground, where the chemicals seeped into the soil. In 1988 an environmental organization told the Nigerian government that local people were at risk, and the government asked the Italians to take the waste away. It was loaded on a boat called the *Karin B*, but no one else would accept the ship's load. Finally the *Karin B* returned to Italy. This episode highlighted the problem of dealing with **toxic waste**.

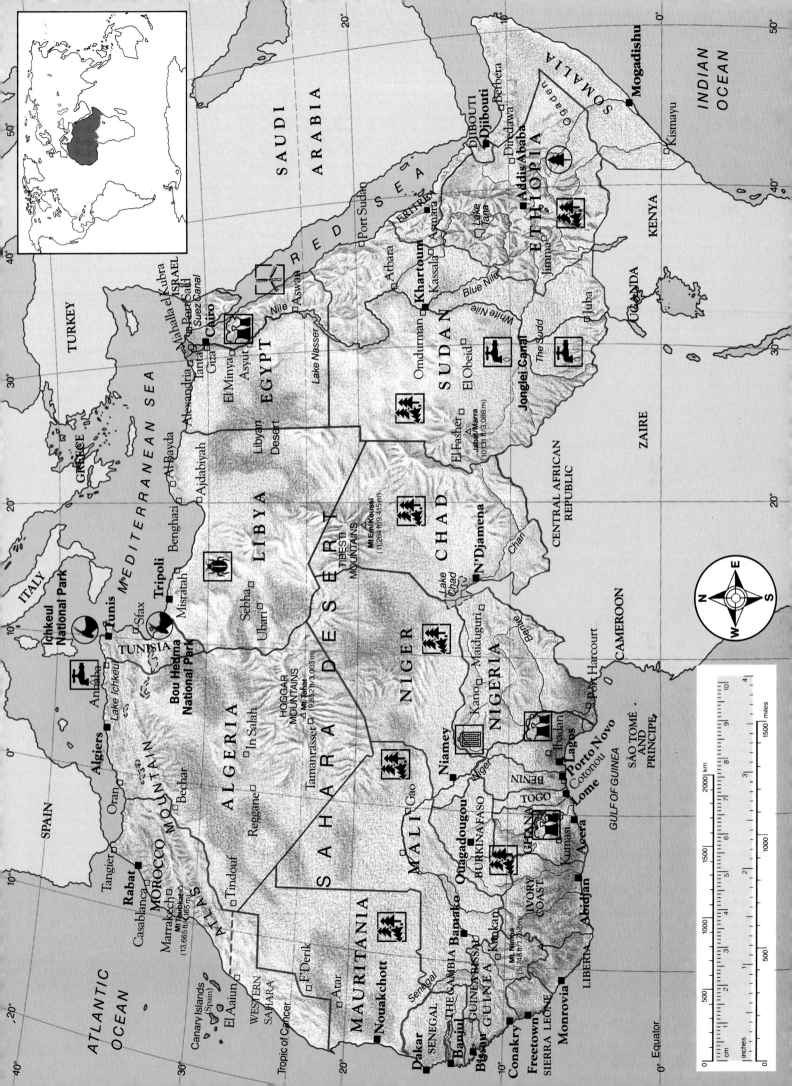

This part of Africa is one of the richest and most productive regions on earth. There are tropical forests, rolling open grasslands, hot deserts and vast rivers and lakes. Much of the region has been exploited and the natural resources often badly managed. But other areas, such as the forests of Zaire and the Kalahari Desert, remain untouched. Human beings would probably have exploited more of this region, but the tsetse fly and other disease-carrying animals have affected how much the continent has been developed.

▼ OKAVANGO DELTA

Thousands of different kinds of animals live in this unique wetland region. But the whole ecosystem, like other wetland areas around the world, may be drained to create more agricultural land to grow cash crops. The need for money often leads governments to make bad decisions about how to use natural resources. The Okavango delta, if protected, could bring in money from tourism.

▲ FUELWOOD FOLLY

In developing countries, where the standard of living is often poor, many people have to search for their fuel. The most easily available fuel is wood, which can be collected from the surrounding countryside.

In Tanzania alone, wood provides 80 percent of the country's total energy needs. Trees are cut down on a large scale, and without their roots there is nothing to hold the soil in place and stop it being eroded. In heavy rain the soil is washed away, and in dry conditions it is blown away by the wind. Slowly the land turns into desert. In this way, the environment is destroyed and a valuable resource is lost.

CHAD

SUDAN

NIGERIA

ETHIOPIA

10°

10°

SOMALIA

Lake Chad

ADAMAOUA MOUNTAINS

Mount Cameroon
(13,353ft/4,070m)

CENTRAL AFRICAN
REPUBLIC

Garamba National Park

CAMEROON

Douala

Bangui

Uele

Yaounde

Malabo

Zaire

UGANDA

Marsabit
Game Reserve

Lake
Turkana

EQUATORIAL
GUINEA

Kampala

KENYA

Odzala
National Park

Kisangani
Boyoma Falls

Kisumu

Libreville

GABON

Masai Mara National Park

Mount
Kenya
(17,058ft/5,200m)

Equator

SÃO TOMÉ
AND
PRINCIPE

ZAIRE

Bukavu

RWANDA

Nairobi

Kigali

Brazzaville

Bujumbura
BURUNDI

Pointe Noire

Kinshasa

Mbuji-Maya

Lake
Tanganyika

Serengeti National Park

Mombasa

CABINDA
(Angola)

Matadi

Kananga

TANZANIA

Zanzibar

Dodoma

INDIAN
OCEAN

Dar es Salaam

Luanda

Kwango

Kasai

Lualaba

Aldabra

ATLANTIC
OCEAN

Tsaso National Park

Likasi

ANGOLA

Lubumbashi

Lake
Bangweula

Lake
Malawi

Njika Plateau National Park

Moroni

COMOROS

Lobito

Huambo

Kitwe

Ruvuma

Antseranana

Porto Alexandre
National Park

ZAMBIA

MALAWI

Lilongwe

Cubango

Lusaka

Zambezi

Kafue National Park

Harare

Moçambique

MADAGASCAR

NAMIBIA

Okavango
Swamp

Victoria
Falls

ZIMBABWE

Mutare

Beira

Toamasina

Francistown

Antananarivo

Windhoek

BOTSWANA

Limpopo

MOZAMBIQUE CHANNEL

20°

MOZAMBIQUE

KALAHARI

Kalahari Gemsbok National Park

DESERT

Gaborone

Kruger National Park

Maputo

Tropic of Capricorn

Namib

Johannesburg

Pretoria

Mbabane
SWAZILAND

REPUBLIC

OF

Vaal

Desert

Kimberley

Welkom

Maseru

Pietermaritzburg

WALVIS BAY
(South Africa)

Bloemfontein

LESOTHO

Durban

Orange

DRAKENSBERG MOUNTAINS

30°

SOUTH AFRICA

Addo Elephant National Park

East London

Cape Town

Cape of
Good Hope

Port Elizabeth

10°

0°

10°

20°

30°

▲ PLANT PHARMACY

The Madagascar periwinkle is a wild plant found on the island of Madagascar. It is now grown all over the world because it produces chemicals used in drugs to cure some diseases, such as cancers of the blood. Around 16.5 tons of periwinkle leaves are needed to make just 28 g (.98 oz) of the chemical. But the chemical is so effective that, for instance, only 4.5 kg (9.9 lb) are needed each year to treat people in the US.

The world is full of plants that may be used to help people. Some have not even been discovered yet. This example shows how important it is to protect natural environments around the world and the variety of plants and animals that live in them.

DRIED FISH AND DESERT

In 1964 a fish called the Nile perch was introduced into Lake Victoria, one of Africa's largest lakes. The fish can grow to 250 kg (550 lb) in size and is worth a lot of money. It is the most common fish in the lake today. But the Nile perch has killed 200 of the lake's 300 other types of fish, many of which could be found only in Lake Victoria. These other fish provided local people with a source of protein and could simply be dried in the sun to prepare them for eating. The Nile perch, on the other hand, has oily flesh and has to be smoked over wood fires. Much of the woodland around the lake has been cut down to build fires for smoking, and the area has been turned into a desert wasteland. Although the Nile perch sells for a lot of money, it has changed the natural environment of the lake and the land around it.

▼ NATIONAL PARKS

Africa is famous for its impressive national parks. These are areas where people and wildlife should be able to live together without harming one another. In Kenya, Tanzania, South Africa, Zambia and Zimbabwe there are vast open spaces where animals roam wild, yet remain protected. But even in such places the wildlife is not absolutely safe. Because of illegal hunting, some species, such as the black rhinoceros, are still at risk.

These national parks are important because tourists from all over the world come to look at the animals and spend their money in Africa. Parks are one way of keeping safe some of Africa's natural resources. The wildlife is protected and the country makes money at the same time.

CATTLE AT RISK

In Africa many people breed their own domestic animals. This can cause problems because many of the breeds are weak and have little **genetic variation**.

In particular, cattle have been dying of a disease called trypanosomiasis, against which they have little resistance. The cost of the disease is estimated at $5 billion every year in lost meat production, and affects 160 million animals in 36 African countries.

But there is a breed of cattle called N'Dama, which has lived in Africa for thousands of years. This breed has developed a resistance to trypanosomiasis. Interbreeding the N'Dama with other cattle may increase the natural resistance of all African cattle to this particular disease.

▲ CASH CROPS

There is enough land in Africa to feed the whole population. But there are problems when vast areas are used to grow food for sale abroad. Crops such as coffee and tea are grown on land that could be used to grow cassava and sorghum plants, the staple diet of the African people. Most of the land is owned by a few landowners, and local people have to farm **marginal land**, which cannot sustain so many people. As a result the land and soil become unfit for growing crops and grazing animals. People then have to farm even more marginal land. This puts increasing pressure on the land, a major natural resource.

▼ MINERAL WEALTH

Some countries in this region are rich in many different kinds of minerals. Minerals are a non-renewable resource, limited to supplies already in the earth. They will eventually be used up. Minerals are an important part of many goods that are made and sold in the world.

Perhaps the mineral worth the most money is gold, and South Africa is the world's biggest producer. South Africa also produces other minerals such as chromium, manganese, platinum and antimony. Zambia and Zaire produce copper and cobalt. Environmental problems are often caused when people mine for minerals. The landscape may be ruined by spoil heaps poisoned with chemicals. This is a particular problem when harmful chemicals are used to extract the minerals.

KILLER SOAP

In Africa there is a plant that produces the endod berry. People use it to make soap to wash themselves and their clothes. Many people wash in the river, and it was discovered that the soap was killing watersnails farther downstream. Nothing else in the river was harmed.

Usually this kind of pollution might be a problem, but the snails that were dying carry a disease called schistosomiasis. This disease kills about 200,000 people in Africa every year. The discovery that the soap was killing the snails may help to control the disease.

This region was once a center of early civilization. The fertile soil, fed by the silt from the Euphrates and Tigris rivers, encouraged people to settle there to grow and store their own food. More recently the discovery of vast amounts of oil turned poor, mainly agricultural nations into rich and powerful countries overnight. In the 1970s these nations put strict limits on selling their oil to other countries. The rest of the world began to explore other sources of energy and looked again at how to manage energy resources throughout the world.

▲ EARLY DOMESTICATION

The Fertile Crescent, in Southwest Asia, was one of the first places in which people began to grow plants and farm animals. The first farmers selected the plants they needed and tethered wild goats and sheep to stop them wandering. Between 7000 and 5000 BC, crops such as wheat, barley, lentils and peas were first farmed.

Since then people have continued to grow new varieties of crops. But recently this natural variation has been reduced and only a few breeds of plants and animals now supply the world with food.

OIL IN STORE

More than half the world's oil reserves are in Southwest Asia. Most of the oil is carried to other countries by pipelines and supertankers. Oil is a fossil fuel made from tiny creatures that lived in the oceans millions of years ago. It is a non-renewable resource and will eventually run out. Because it is so valuable, people are constantly looking for new reserves all over the world.

▼ OIL POLLUTION

War has caused much of the oil pollution in the Persian Gulf. During the war between Iran and Iraq (1980–1988), oil tankers and oil refineries were attacked by both sides. When Iraq invaded Kuwait in 1990 it set alight oil wells. The oil spills this caused damaged the environment. In time the habitat and wildlife will recover, but the effects of oil pollution were devastating.

The Commonwealth of Independent States (CIS) together make up one of the largest political entities in the world. The region has vast natural resources. There are millions of acres of forests and wide-open grasslands suitable for growing wheat and other cereal crops.

There are valuable minerals, in particular huge reserves of fossil fuels such as coal, oil and natural gas. But these resources have been badly managed. In some regions there has also been considerable waste and pollution by industry.

▲ ARAL SEA

Perhaps "arid sea" is a better name, because this huge lake in Russia is rapidly drying up. Water from the rivers that feed the lake has been used to irrigate cotton fields in the region. The land around the lake has become a desert. Since 1960 the edge of the lake has moved back by about 80 km (50 mi), and each year the water level drops more than 3 ft. This is changing the region's climate because the sea helped to moderate extreme changes of temperature. Now the summers are hotter and the winters are colder than before. The Aral Sea will never be the same again because too much water has been taken from it.

▼ POLLUTION PROBLEMS

Between 1983 and 1988 there was a huge increase of pesticides in the Sea of Azov. In the Volga-Caspian basin pollution levels are also increasing. This is where most of the world's sturgeon, the fish from which caviar comes, live. Each year 403,700 tons of organic waste, 14,300 tons of oily waste, 49,500 tons of nitrogen and 22,000 tons of phosphorus end up in the Volga. These chemicals are all washed into the sea.

RADIATION SICKNESS

Unlike the industrial towns to the south and north, the air and water in Muslimova appear to be clear and clean. But a nuclear reprocessing and waste plant has been causing pollution in the area for over 40 years. Water from Lake Karachai that should have supplied 124,000 people was slowly polluted over this time. The waste that was dumped in the lake made the water radioactive. The lake has now dried up, and the radioactive dust from the bottom of the lake has been blown over an area of 880 sq mi. There are 41,000 people living in this region, and the pollution has made many of them ill.

Pollution from nuclear industry is difficult to see, but the damage it does to the environment and its people is often clear enough.

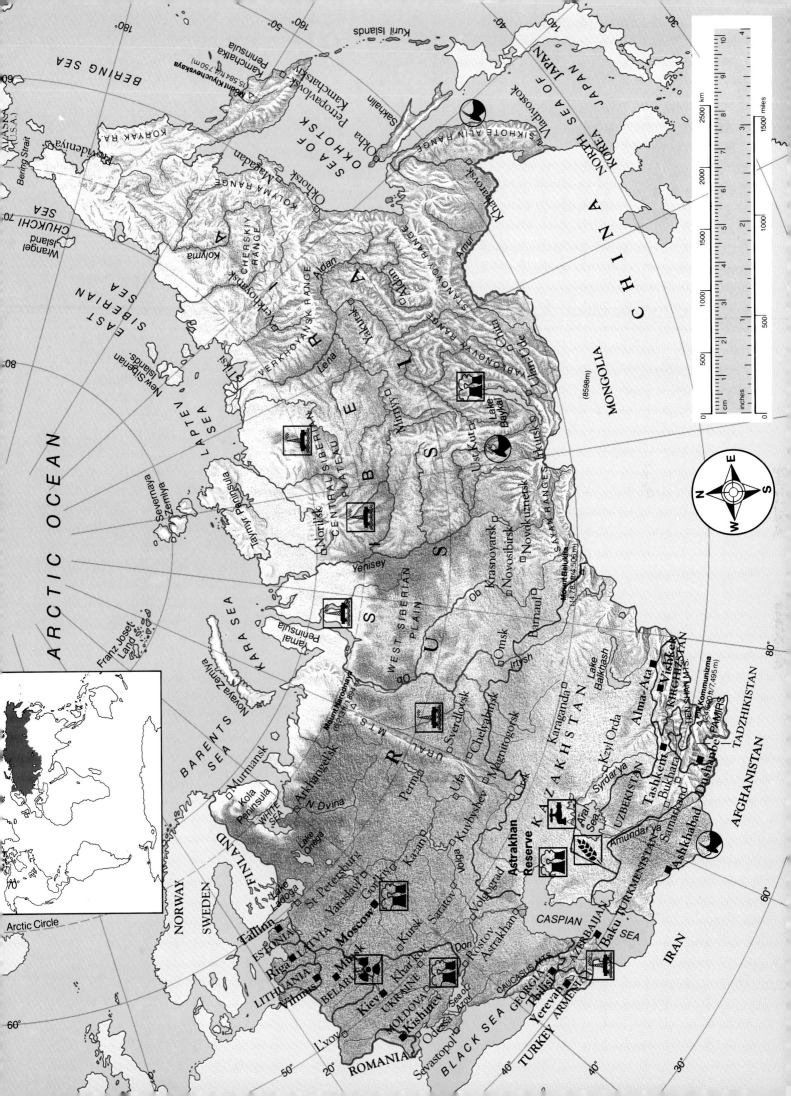

In this region of the world the environment comes under pressure because of a large population. For instance, the demand for wood to meet people's fuel needs has led to cutting down trees on a large scale. Several large dam-building projects have been developed that use natural hydropower, but the immense size of the projects means that some of them have created their own environmental problems. On the other hand, some kinds of modern technology, such as bio-gas digesters that use human and animal wastes to make gas and fertilizers, have worked very effectively in rural communities in this region.

FROG'S LEGS ▶

The rice fields in India were once full of bullfrogs. They enjoyed the damp living conditions and the regular supply of insects that were attracted to the rice crop. But the bullfrogs themselves began to be harvested in their thousands. They were valuable for their legs, which were served in expensive European restaurants. Although some people made money from this harvest, it created two problems. First, the insect pests were no longer kept under control by the frogs and ate the rice crop, reducing the annual rice harvest. Second, more people began to suffer from malaria. This is a disease spread by some types of mosquito, a favorite food for the frogs. Sometimes, upsetting the balance of the environment has a hidden cost.

AID

Many developed countries give aid to others. Sometimes they plan major projects to help the people of a developing country. For example, money was provided for the Amlohri opencut coal mine in Uttar Pradesh. But a visiting team of advisers to the mine found the countryside devastated by fires. There was also severe pollution from dust and gas. Countries who offer help have to understand the effects such a scheme may have on a region. They must make sure that they pass on all the information needed by local people, so that the project can be continued by them without harming the environment.

▼ POVERTY TRAP

People who have very little depend more than others on their immediate environment to supply their needs. On the hills of Nepal people have cut down trees for firewood. Without the trees' roots to hold it in place, the soil has been washed away by the rains. The water then has no soil to absorb it, so more rain runs into the rivers, which flood. This happens in many parts of the world and shows how poverty often creates more problems for the poor.

CHINA AND JAPAN AND THEIR NEIGHBORS

China is a vast country, the third largest in the world. It is quickly becoming industrialized, and this is creating problems for the natural environment. China has a population of over 1.1 billion people, which represents a huge human energy resource. But in the mid-1980s, an attempt to house more people meant the loss of much farmland. Japan has very few natural resources but has become one of the most successful industrialized nations in the world. It uses resources from other countries to make its products. This industry has created environmental problems, and Japan is increasingly concerned about such issues.

THE MURKY YELLOW RIVER ▶

All rivers carry some mud and silt to the sea. But the Yellow River carries more than a billion tons of soil each year. The river bed is now so high that it runs 3 to 10 meters (9.9 – 33 ft) above the land along a channel enclosed by raised banks on either side. When the river floods, people are drowned and crops are ruined.

The soil comes from the hillsides, where bad farming has caused severe erosion. About 172,000 sq mi of China's Loess Plateau has been turned to bare rock and 71.5 tons of soil is lost from 2.5 acres each year. So much soil is washed into the river that in places it is liquid mud. To help this, small dams have been built across gulleys, and the surface water is trapped so that it does not remove soil and wash it into the river.

▼ CHINESE MEDICINES

For thousands of years the Chinese have used plants and animals to treat sick people, and many of these medicines work very well. But the demand for drugs that use parts of animals has put some species at risk. All species of rhinoceros are hunted. This is because the rhinoceros' horn is an ingredient in a much valued drug in China. The tiger is also hunted by poachers for its bones. In China tiger bones are ground up and used to make tiger bone wine, which is drunk as a tonic. Because people are prepared to pay high prices for these products, the existence of rare animals continues to be threatened.

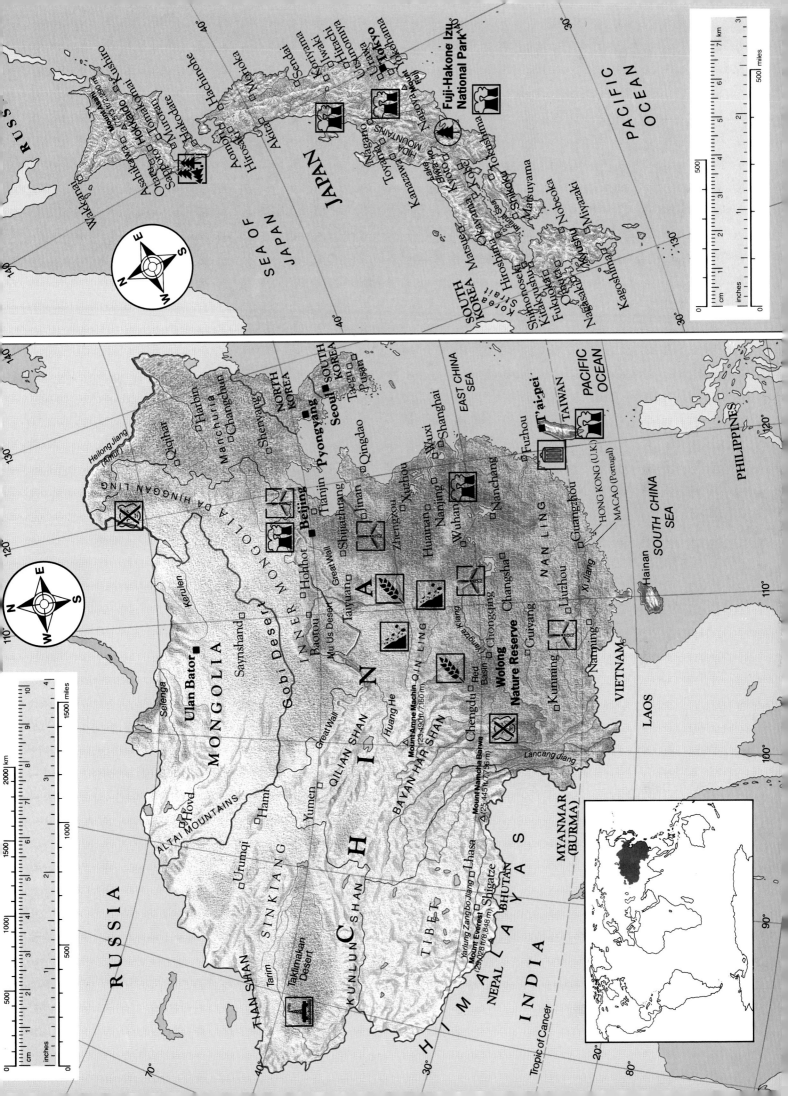

HYDROELECTRIC SCHEMES

All over the world the energy from falling water is transformed into electricity. It is a clean and natural source of energy, yet when large dams are built as part of this process, they can bring their own problems. Land may be flooded, and people lose their homes. Dams may silt up and there is an increase in water-carried diseases such as malaria and bilharzia. Today in China, over 90,000 small-scale dams have been built. Between them they produce more than 5,000 megawatts of electricity – as much as six nuclear power stations. The small dams are appropriate for the region and reduce the impact of the dams on the environment.

◀ POWER TO THE PEOPLE

China has a huge potential for energy production, but always needs even more energy. China is the world's second largest producer of coal, and has an oil and gas reserve in the Tarim Basin bigger than France. As its industries develop, China will need to use all its available energy resources. There are now plans to build the Three Gorges Dam on the River Yangtze. The dam will flood one of the most beautiful regions of China, and more than one million people will have to leave their homes. Although the dam will provide energy, its effect on the environment will be enormous and this must be taken into account.

TAIWAN POLLUTION

Taiwan is a successful country where industry has grown and thrived. But, as so often happens, because the country has developed so quickly there are now major pollution problems. Heavy metals, such as cadmium, chromium, zinc and lead, have been found in crop-growing land close to factories and industrial waste dumps. Of the 17 rivers in Taiwan, 14 are polluted, five seriously. The industrial region of Taipei suffers from severe air pollution. In 1989 the air registered 188 on the Pollution Standard Index, higher than the figure of 165 recorded for Los Angeles smogs in the 1960s. Where there is successful industrial development there is always an environmental cost. Countries need to deal with this at an early stage to avoid even bigger problems in the future.

In 1993 Japan hosted an international conference on wetland conservation. At the same time the government had plans to build a huge canal that would threaten Lake Utonai. This lake is one of four important rare wetland sites in Japan. The canal, known as the Chitose River Channel, would control flooding in Hokkaido and would take up to 30 years to build. But it would also cut off the river that supplies water to Lake Utonai. Fishermen who use the Pacific coast are worried that water running off from this canal will spoil their fishing grounds. If the region floods, the water would be full of silt, dirt and chemicals. Such huge projects can have a devastating effect on the natural environment.

ACID RAIN GAIN

Japan is suffering from increased levels of acid rain, which is affecting the plants and wildlife in its lakes and rivers. Research suggests that 35 percent of the sulfur that makes up the acid rain comes from Japan, but that 50 percent comes from China and the remaining 15 percent from Korea. The main cause of sulfur in the atmosphere is coal burning, and China is the world's biggest consumer of coal.

Like Canada and some northern European countries, Japan is suffering from acid rain that has been created by industry in other countries.

▲ A NUCLEAR FUTURE?

Japan has few natural energy resources of its own, and so has invested a great deal of money into developing nuclear energy. In 1992 the Japanese ship *Akatsuki Maru* left France carrying a ton of plutonium to fuel Japan's new fast-breeder reactors. These were planned to replace the usual nuclear reactors that provided most of the country's nuclear energy. Many countries felt that carrying such a large amount of plutonium over such a long distance was dangerous, because of the risk of accident or terrorism. The plutonium was safely delivered, but Japan is now unsure about using it in a fast-breeder reactor. The first experimental one opened at Monju in 1994. Japan may be the only country to build such reactors. Most other countries have canceled their fast-breeder programs.

TECHNOLOGICAL SOLUTIONS

In the 1950s and 1960s Japan's young and rapidly growing industries were causing pollution in the atmosphere, rivers and agricultural land. In Minamata people were poisoned by fish that had absorbed mercury from the rivers in which they lived. In Yokkaichi people suffered from asthma caused by heavily polluted air. Today ways are being found to reduce the pollution. Japan has developed a process that removes chemicals such as sulfur and nitric acid from factory waste. The units that carry out this process are being used in much of Japan's industry. They make up three-quarters of all such units in the world. This same technology is available for China and other fast-developing countries.

Southeast Asia has large areas of tropical forest, one of the region's main resources. Unfortunately this resource is not managed in a sustainable way. Many of the slow-growing tropical hardwood trees are being cut down at an alarming rate.

Each year 875 million cubic feet of hardwood are taken from Sarawak alone. Demand for hardwood trees may be reduced by the end of the 1990s, and in ten years time Sarawak may have to buy its timber from other countries.

PEST CONTROL

In Indonesia farmers found that they were able to grow two crops of rice instead of just one a year. They achieved this by planting particular kinds of rice and using fertilizers and pesticides. But they had to spray crops with insecticides up to eight times in the growing season to keep an insect pest, called the brown hopper, under control. The insecticides were expensive and the hoppers continued to cause a problem. Scientists found that the chemicals were killing spiders, the hoppers' natural enemy.

The answer was an "integrated pest management" system (IPM). Farmers stopped spraying chemicals and were trained to conserve natural predators such as the spiders. After three years farmers were using less pesticide, growing more rice and doing less damage to their environment.

▲ TERRIBLE TRADE

Wild animals are a resource like any other in the world. In the Philippines, Taiwan, Thailand, Indonesia and Singapore people trade in wild animals. They are collected to sell as pets or for research. Parrots, monkeys, fish, and reptiles such as lizards and snakes are all collected and sold. Some trade is legal, and collectors, exporters and importers all have a special licence. But there is still a great deal of illegal trade. A constant demand for wild animals threatens natural populations of even quite common animals.

Worldwide 50,000 primates, 4 million birds and 350 million tropical fish are bought and sold. Many more animals die when they are taken from one place to another, or are killed during their capture.

▼ SWEET SUFFOCATION

In March 1992 there was a leak of 9,900 tons of molasses from a sugar factory into the Nam Phong River in Thailand. This has affected 600 km (375 mi) of river, starving the water of oxygen and suffocating the fish and other living things. The pollution spread to two other rivers and for each 0.625 mi of water contaminated, about half a ton of fish died. For the local communities in the area, who rely on the fish as a source of food, the accident has been a disaster.

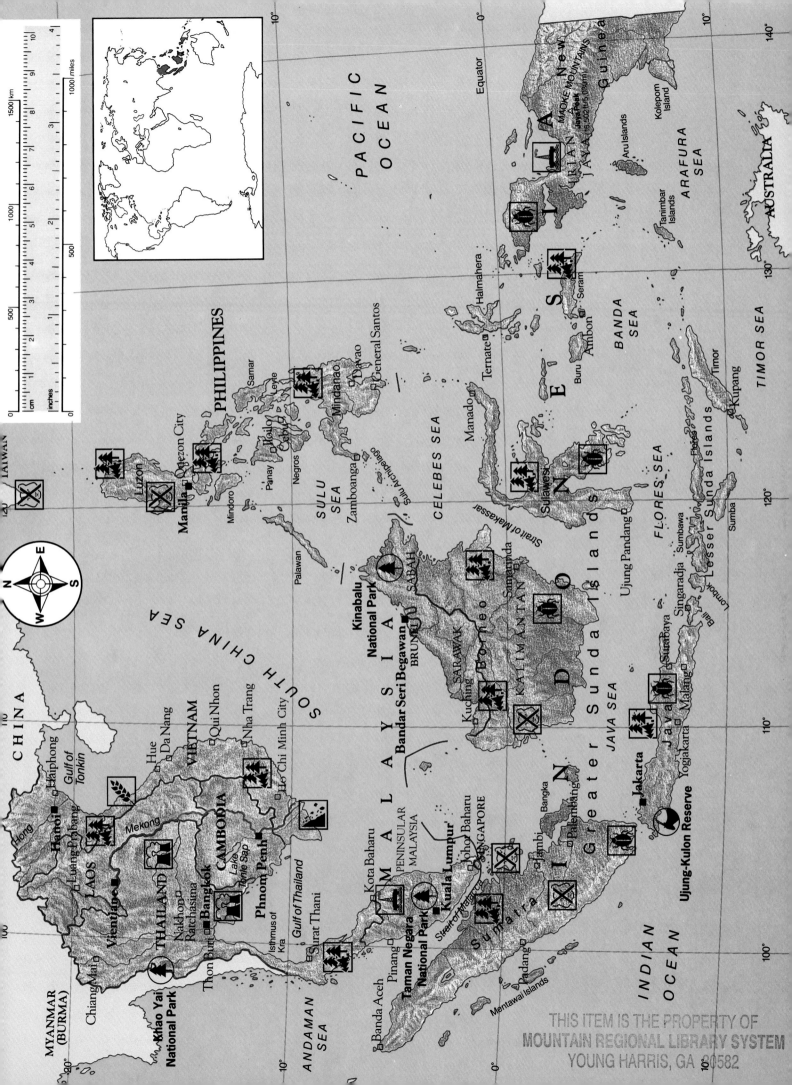

MYANMAR
(BURMA)

CHINA

Chiang Mai

Hong

Luang Prabang
Vientiane
LAOS
Nakhon Ratchasima
THAILAND
Bangkok
Thon Buri

Khao Yai
National Park

Mekong

CAMBODIA
Lake Tonle Sap
Phnom Penh

Surat Thani

Isthmus of Kra

Gulf of Thailand

Haiphong
Gulf of Tonkin
Hanoi

Hue
Da Nang
Qui Nhon
VIETNAM
Nha Trang
Ho Chi Minh City

SOUTH CHINA SEA

ANDAMAN SEA

Banda Aceh

Kota Baharu

Pinang

PENINSULAR MALAYSIA

Taman Negara
National Park

Kuala Lumpur
Johor Baharu
SINGAPORE

Strait of Malacca

Sumatra

Padang

Mentawai Islands

Jambi
Palembang
Bangka

INDIAN OCEAN

Jakarta
Ujung-Kulon Reserve

Yogyakarta
Surabaya
Malang
Java
Greater Sunda Islands

JAVA SEA

Bali
Lombok
Lesser Sunda Islands
Singaradja
Sumbawa
Sumba
Flores

PHILIPPINES

Luzon
Quezon City
Manila
Mindoro

Samar
Leyte
Iloilo
Cebu
Panay
Negros

Palawan

SULU SEA

Zamboanga
Sulu Archipelago

Mindanao
Davao
General Santos

CELEBES SEA

Kinabalu National Park
SABAH
BRUNEI
Bandar Seri Begawan
SARAWAK
Kuching
Borneo
KALIMANTAN
Samarinda

Strait of Makassar

INDONESIA

PACIFIC OCEAN

Manado

Ternate
Halmahera

Buru
Seram
Ambon

CELEBES

Sulawesi

Ujung Pandang

BANDA SEA

Timor

IRIAN New
MAOKE MOUNTAINS
Jaya Peak
16,502 ft (5,030 m)

Kolepom Island

Aru Islands

Tanimbar Islands

ARAFURA SEA

Kupang

TIMOR SEA

AUSTRALIA

TAIWAN

Equator

0°
10°
20°
100°
110°
120°
130°
140°

1500 km
1000 miles
1000
500
500

N
W E
S

AUSTRALIA AND NEW ZEALAND

Australia is a vast continent made up of mainly dry or desert lands, rich in mineral resources. Much of the land is used for livestock farming, but drought is a constant problem. In contrast, New Zealand has a much wetter, cooler climate, which provides high-quality grazing land for sheep farming. Both countries have supplies of gas and coal as well as hydroelectricity. New Zealand also uses geothermal energy. People are increasingly aware of the need to protect the countries' environments, with their unique species of plants and animals.

BIOLOGICAL DISASTER ▶

In the 1930s a pest called the cane grub attacked Australia's sugar cane plantations. To control this pest a predator of the cane grub, the cane (or marine) toad, was brought to Queensland from South America. Unfortunately the toad also started to eat food other than the cane grub, such as amphibians and birds native to Australia. The cane grub remains a problem and the cane toad has become an even bigger problem. It is spreading through the tropical part of Australia, endangering the existence of the local wildlife wherever it settles.

Introducing animals or plants from one part of the world into new areas can often upset the balance of nature and reduce the biodiversity of a country rather than increase it.

UNIQUE SPECIES

When Europeans first came to New Zealand they brought with them their own domestic animals, such as sheep and goats. They also brought red deer and rabbits to remind them of their original home in Europe. These changes affected the natural environment. The original grasses of South Island have disappeared because of intensive farming and overgrazing and have been replaced by weaker, introduced grasses. Such changes reduce the land's value as a resource for the people.

▼ SALTY SOIL

About 70 percent of Australia is semi-desert or arid land. About half of this is used to farm sheep and cattle. Nearly a fifth is unfit for use because of **salination**.

This has been caused by farmers who have cut down trees and scrub plants to plant grasses to feed their livestock. The trees and scrub plants absorbed the salt in the soil. Forest fires also burned away the salt that built up in the plants. Because the new grasses could not stop the salt sinking deep into the underground water system, the land became very salty. The grasses could not grow in these conditions, and the land became unfit for livestock too.

New trees have been planted to absorb the salt. Over many years the natural balance may be restored.

Many of the islands in the Pacific Ocean are formed from lava from volcanoes that start on the seabed. When the rock from the lava breaks down, it makes a rich soil. Seeds from plants such as the coconut palm drift or blow on to the islands and grow there. Their isolation from the mainland means that the islands' environment is easily harmed by change. Their limited natural resources must be managed carefully to keep them safe for the future.

HAWAIIAN GOOSE ▶

Early European settlers who explored the world took with them domestic animals such as pigs, goats, cats and, unintentionally, rats. The effect these animals had on the wildlife of the places they visited was often disastrous. All over the Pacific Islands, they caused problems, killing or competing with the island animals. Rats ate the eggs of birds. Cats chased and killed birds and other animals, many of which had lost their natural fear of being hunted. In particular the Hawaiian goose was hunted by rats and cats. The goose was also hunted by whalers for food supplies on board the whaling ships. At the beginning of the 18th century there were about 25,000 geese. By 1969 only 35 were left in the wild. But the geese have been bred in captivity and are now being reintroduced in the wild.

GALAPAGOS TOMATO

There is a great variety of plants and animals in the world. And there are many species that can adapt to changes in their environment. This variety can be helpful to people.

On the shores of the Galapagos Islands there is a wild type of tomato that can grow in saltwater. The genes from this plant have been added to farmed, or cultivated, tomatoes. Now the cultivated tomatoes can be watered with one-third sea water and grow in conditions that would kill other tomatoes.

▼ THE PRICE OF GOLD

Since the 1980s, gold has become an important resource in Papua New Guinea. On Lihir Island there are 1,460.8 tons of gold deposits, the largest found outside South Africa. But because the island is so remote, most of the waste materials from the mining end up in its rivers. In the process of gold mining, over nine years one mine can produce about 309,100 tons of copper, 41,800 tons of cadmium, 10,340 lb of mercury, as well as lead, zinc, iron and arsenic. This waste is dumped into the environment.

Mineral extraction creates severe pollution, and in some places, such as tropical forests, it can be especially destructive.

The Arctic is an ocean surrounded on all sides by the northern shores of the three continents of North America, Asia and Europe. The region has always been exploited. In the Middle Ages sailors hunted a small whale, called the narwhal, for the male's single tusk, which was sold as unicorn horn. By 1650 Russia was making a third of its income from selling the fur of the Siberian wolf. Today the Arctic is exploited for oil. Parts of the Arctic Ocean are also rich fishing grounds producing around a tenth of the world's annual fish catch.

OIL SPOIL ▶

On March 24, 1989, an accident at Prince William Sound, Alaska, was responsible for one of the world's biggest oil spills. The supertanker *Exxon Valdez* ran aground, spilling 39,600 tons of oil into the sea. The oil spread along 2,000 km (1,250 mi) of shoreline causing terrible pollution in a region of great natural beauty. Between March and September, 36,000 sea birds, 1,000 sea otters and 153 eagles were killed by the oil.

But, as with other oil spills, although the immediate disaster was devastating, the damage was not permanent. In the space of a few years the environment often recovers and the wildlife begins to increase. Oil pollution is harmful, but compared with other forms of pollution, such as pesticides, it is not as damaging in the long-term.

FUR CRAZY ▶

The Arctic has been an important resource for hunters for many years. The Hudson Bay trading company became a center for buying and selling the skins of Arctic animals, such as the fox, lynx, beaver and hare.

These Arctic animals have thick fur to protect them from the freezing temperatures. Because of this, they were especially valuable, and their skins were sold for clothing in North America and Europe.

In the 1980s, in some countries, fur from hunted animals became unfashionable, because it was seen as part of a cruel trade. But today this trade continues. In Canada and Scandinavia people are still hunting seal pups for their skins, and the fur traders are still making a lot of money. So as long as there is a market for natural fur the trade will continue.

The seas around Antarctica are rich in nutrients that the ocean currents carry to the surface from the seabed. These nutrients feed large populations of a few species. The first people to exploit the Antarctic were sealers, who by the end of the 19th century had hunted the fur seals almost to extinction. Scientists believe that the landmass contains over 900 important mineral deposits and that there is oil in the region too. Antarctica remains undisturbed for the moment. But this could change at any time.

WHALE WASTE ▶

In the early 1900s, hunting whales was big business. Modern factory ships almost destroyed the entire population of the largest species, the blue whale. The whale was valued for its meat and for the oil from its body, which was used in manufacturing. The island of South Georgia became the center of the whaling industry, and in the summer season of 1930/31 over 29,000 blue whales were killed.

The hunting of the blue whale was made illegal in the Southern Hemisphere in 1965. Today only a handful of nations, including Japan, Norway and Russia, continue to hunt whales. This should be for research and scientific purposes only.

This example shows how money is often considered more important than the protection of a renewable resource, in this case the blue whale.

▼ A SAFE FUTURE?

Antarctica has an unusual status in the world. Although people have often exploited its oceans, the landmass has remained fairly free of pollution and exploitation. Several countries claim to own parts of it, but plans for developing its natural resources have not been carried out. This is because countries have agreed to cooperate in managing the Antarctic. Scientists believe that research in the region could be used to help the whole world. From research in Antarctica they discovered a hole in the ozone layer.

The Antarctic Treaty was drawn up to keep the spirit of cooperation alive. But if people discover oil or other valuable resources, the region may yet be overexploited.

KRILL KILL

The blue whale has been hunted in the Antarctic over many years and its numbers have been greatly reduced. This means that the tiny shrimp-like krill, which are the whales' main food, have been able to breed, without any important natural predator. There are now such large numbers of krill that they have themselves become a new resource. They are hunted as a source of food by the Japanese.

The number of krill in the Antarctic is probably greater than the annual harvest of all the shellfish in the world's other oceans. During 1980 over 440,000 tons of krill were harvested. Now no one knows if there will be enough krill left to feed the whales. People are always ready to adapt and exploit new resources. But in doing so there is often a cost to the environment.

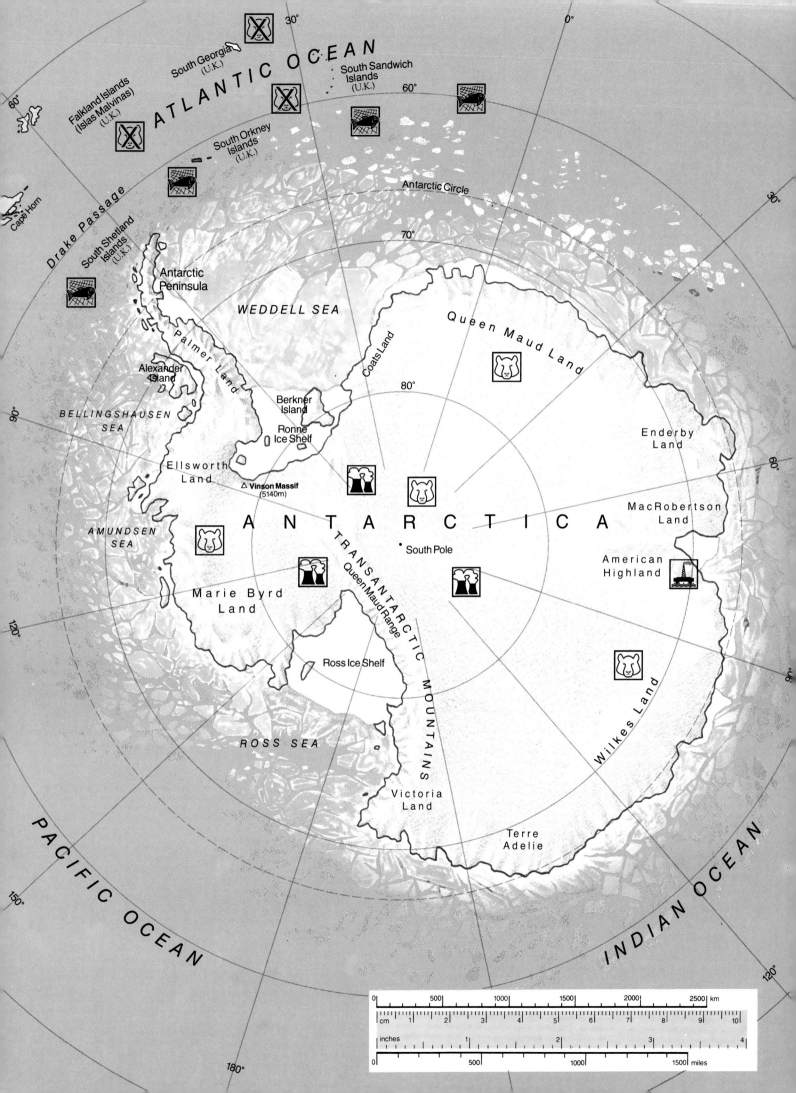

ATLANTIC OCEAN

30°

0°

South Georgia
(U.K.)

Falkland Islands
(Islas Malvinas)
(U.K.)

South Sandwich
Islands
(U.K.)

60°

South Orkney
Islands
(U.K.)

Antarctic Circle

Cape Horn

Drake Passage

70°

South Shetland
Islands (U.K.)

Antarctic
Peninsula

WEDDELL SEA

Queen Maud Land

0°

30°

Palmer
Land

Coats Land

Alexander
Island

BELLINGSHAUSEN
SEA

Berkner
Island

Ronne
Ice Shelf

80°

Enderby
Land

96°

Ellsworth
Land

△ Vinson Massif
(5140m)

ANTARCTICA

MacRobertson
Land

60°

AMUNDSEN
SEA

• South Pole

American
Highland

120°

Marie Byrd
Land

TRANSANTARCTIC
Queen Maud Range

90°

Ross Ice Shelf

MOUNTAINS

Wilkes Land

ROSS SEA

Victoria
Land

PACIFIC OCEAN

150°

Terre
Adelie

INDIAN OCEAN

180°

120°

0	500	1000	1500	2000	2500 km

cm	1	2	3	4	5	6	7	8	9	10

inches	1	2	3	4

0	500	1000	1500 miles

GLOSSARY AND FURTHER INFORMATION

Here are some simple explanations of the main terms used in this book.

Algal blooms Large collections of plants called algae that feed on pollution and spread rapidly. As the algae dies it rots, which uses up oxygen in the water and allows poisons to build up.

Cash crops Crops, such as coffee or sugar beet, that are grown for sale to other countries rather than for the people in the country where they are grown.

Developing world A term used to describe countries that rely more on money from agriculture, such as growing cash crops, than on manufacturing.

Ecosystem A natural system based on the relationship between the physical environment and living things in a particular area. A tropical forest is an ecosystem, so are the grasslands or savannas of Africa.

Exploited All natural resources are developed and used by people. Over exploitation of a natural resource often damages the environment.

Genetic material Genetic material, or the pattern of genes, contains the information that shapes the appearance of every living thing. When a species of plant or animal becomes extinct, unique genetic material is lost forever.

Genetic variation This refers to the differences between living things. A species can contain several groups that differ from each other. Some groups develop differences to help them survive changing conditions.

Hardwood A slow-growing, dense wood that comes mainly from deciduous trees, such as oak and elm. The word also refers to the trees from which the wood comes. Many rain forest trees, such as mahogany and teak, are hardwoods.

Hydropower Also called hydroelectricity. The use of falling water to drive machinery, which makes electricity.

Industrialized Industrialized countries are those that rely mainly on money from manufacturing, or the use of raw materials to make goods, to sell to others.

Marginal land Land at the edge of cultivated areas that is poor quality and not suitable for agricultural use.

Organic A term to describe something that is living or has lived. Organic waste rots naturally. The word organic can also refer to a method of farming that uses natural waste rather than manufactured chemicals to improve the soil.

Salination The process through which salt builds up in the soil so that crops cannot grow. This usually happens when bad farming causes changes in the water level and salts from deep down in the soil are brought to the surface. It can be caused when irrigation water is taken in by plants, but the salts in the water are left behind. Salt deposits also come from industrial and chemical waste.

Softwood A fast-growing wood that comes mainly from coniferous trees such as pine and cedar. The word also refers to the trees from which the wood comes.

Technological revolution Technology involves using scientific knowledge to make things that have a practical purpose. New technology began to be developed in the second half of the eighteenth century with inventions such as the steam engine. Since then modern technology has created many changes in the world and in the way we live.

Toxic waste Any poisonous waste material. Toxic waste is created by most modern industries and includes everything from untreated sewage to nuclear waste.

Turbine A huge wheel that converts the energy from a moving force, such as wind or water, into another form, often electricity.

Water cycle The continuous recycling of the Earth's water. Water from the seas and rivers evaporates, cools and condenses into clouds and then falls as rain. The rain drains back into the rivers and seas.

Water table The level at which water lies on the land. It may be below or at soil level. When there is a drought or when farmers take too much water for irrigation, the water table is lowered.

Watershed An area, often a high ridge, that divides two rivers and their tributaries from each other. It can also mean the natural sources of fresh water in any area, its lakes, rivers and underground water.

National grid A system that collects the nation's supply of electricity into power stations and then sends it all over the country along power lines to where it is needed.

FURTHER INFORMATION

Here is a selection of organizations that are actively involved in helping to improve the environment and who are making people aware of the problems that threaten it. You can write to these organizations for further information, but please enclose an SASE.

The Sierra Club
730 Polk Street
San Francisco, CA 94109

Friends of the Earth
218 D Street S.E.
Washington, DC 20077-0936
  also
251 Laurier Avenue West
Suite 701
Ottawa, Ontario K1P 5J6

Greenpeace
1436 U Street N.W.
P.O. Box 3720
Washington, DC 20007
  also
185 Spadina Avenue
Toronto, Ontario M5T 2C6

National Audubon Society
950 3rd Avenue
New York, NY 10022
London W6 OLT

Earth Island Institute
301 Broadway
San Francisco, CA 94133

Environmental Defense Fund
257 Park Avenue South
New York, NY 10010

The Wilderness Society
1400 Eye Street N.W.
Washington, DC 20005

MAP INDEX

INDEX OF RESOURCES